SIR WILFRED GRENFELL

BY GENEVIEVE FOX

WITH ILLUSTRATIONS BY
MARY REARDON

New York: Thomas Y. Crowell Company

Designed by GEORGE HORNBY

MANUFACTURED IN THE UNITED STATES OF AMERICA
AMERICAN BOOK–STRATFORD PRESS, INC., NEW YORK

Printing Statement:

Due to the very old age and scarcity of this book, many of the pages may be hard to read due to the blurring of the original text, possible missing pages, missing text and other issues beyond our control.

Because this is such an important and rare work, we believe it is best to reproduce this book regardless of its original condition.

Thank you for your understanding.

They were brothers who had lost track
of each other for years

ACKNOWLEDGMENTS

The author is grateful to the many people who helped her in gathering material for this book. Thanks are due especially to the International Grenfell Association and to the Grenfell Association of America for giving their cooperation, opening their files, and permitting the use of quotations from the magazine, *Among the Deep Sea Fishers*. To those who contributed their personal reminiscences of Sir Wilfred, the author is indebted for many of the new incidents in this biography. Miss Jessie C. Beecher, Miss Eleanor Cushman, Mrs. Elliott Gardner, Rev. Dr. Theodore A. Greene, Wilfred T. Grenfell, Jr., William L. Savage, and Mrs. Wyman Shaw (Rosamond Grenfell) gave generously of their time to talk about him. The snatches of songs are taken from *Ballads and Sea Songs of Newfoundland*, edited by Elizabeth B. Greenleaf and Grace Y. Mansfield, and used with the kind permission of Mrs. Greenleaf. Patricia Knapp's description of a visit to Sir Wilfred is quoted by permission of the Emma Willard School, Troy, N. Y. Various short quotations throughout the book, mainly items of conversation, are quoted from *Forty Years for Labrador* by Wilfred Grenfell, with the permission of the Houghton Mifflin Company.

Contents

vii

Contents

SIR WILFRED GRENFELL

CHAPTER ONE

A Lucky Boy

A great wind blew off the Irish Sea. It sent the tide rushing up the wide, sandy bed of the river Dee, working havoc with the small boats moored along the sea wall, and it shouted and whistled at the sleepy English fishing village on the shore.

"Have you heard the news?" one rubber-booted fisherman asked of another. They had rowed out to double anchor on their sail boats.

The other stopped short in the midst of tightening a knot. News at Parkgate was spiced by its rarity. "No. Nothing 'cept Jim's losing his boat."

The first fisherman grinned and jerked a thumb toward a large, half-timbered house set back a little distance from the wall. " 'Tis a new boy they've got at the big house."

"So-o? By the look o' things, he'll see some rough sailing, he will. My brother Alfred's boy was born just such a day as this, and he—"

"Signs or no signs, this boy's lucky. Better folks never walked the earth than the schoolmaster and his wife, and they've got good blood in their veins, they have."

The old fisherman was right. Wilfred Grenfell, the blue-eyed baby who had just arrived at Mostyn House on that February day in 1865, was fortunate. Perhaps the winds that howled down the chimneys, banged the heavy old doors, and rattled the small-paned leaded windows were just giving a hint that even a boy born in such an out-of-the-world spot as this might see plenty of excitement in the course of his life.

He was lucky to be a son of Algernon and Jane Hutchinson Grenfell.

His father was a brilliant scholar. And he was as kind as he was wise. Wilfred never forgot a children's party under the jasmine and rose bushes in Mostyn House Garden. "Stop throwing that ball so near the windows," warned Father, not once but twice. Wilfred kept on playing dangerously. "Go to the nursery at once and stay there till I call you," ordered Father. It was a bitter, bitter blow for a small boy—to leave the garden, the other children, and worst of all the feast—ripe red strawberries, drenched in heavy cream, and cakes. Mr. Grenfell's afternoon was ruined too, for he knew exactly how Wilfred was feeling. At the end of an hour, he decided that he and his son had been punished enough and escorted the boy back to the garden and to the strawberries and cakes.

What a sense of humor he had! Once when he and Mrs. Grenfell had departed for a vacation on the continent leaving their sons in the care of the housekeeper, the boys promptly dispatched a telegram to a London cousin—"Come down and stay the holidays. Father has gone to Aix." Father, who had by chance stopped off for a night at the home of these same relatives, could not resist wiring back, "Not gone yet. Father." One can fairly hear his chuckles. Of course he saw to it that the cousin went right along to Parkgate.

Looking back as a grown man, Wilfred Grenfell said he couldn't remember ever hearing his mother "speak an angry or unkind word." Her thoughtfulness of others was unfailing. An incident of the boy's preparatory school days is typical. It was the custom for all students to wear buttonhole bouquets on Sunday mornings at chapel. Every single week, during the two years her son was attending this school, a box of flowers arrived by post in time to supply a Sunday boutonniere. Not once did she forget. Not once was she too busy. Yet she carried heavy responsibilities, running a family and helping her husband run a large boys' school.

She was the kind of mother a boy could turn to when he had a hard problem to meet, sure that she would put herself in his place.

These parents gave to Wilfred a healthy body, a fine mind, and other priceless things—a warm heart, tolerance, and a sense of humor that never failed him. They did not coddle him. In a day when fathers and mothers looked after their children overmuch, they encouraged theirs to venture and be self-reliant.

He had the companionship of other boys—a hundred in his father's school besides his three brothers. Yet there were plenty of chances to play by himself when he felt like it. Algernon, the oldest of the four young Grenfells, was his partner from time to time in bold enterprises and also led him into some bad scrapes. With the two younger brothers he had less chance to play, since one lived to be only seven years old and the other was a cripple for several years.

Wilfred was lucky, exceptionally lucky, in his ancestors. On his father's side were doughty Cornishmen who knew not the meaning of the word "fear." There was Sir Richard Grenville, a cousin of Sir Walter Raleigh's. (They spelled the name differently in those days.) With one ship and one hundred and fifty men, he held off for fifteen hours a whole Spanish treasure fleet of fifteen galleons manned by five thousand men. You can read about him in Tennyson's poem *The Revenge*.

Sir Bevil Grenville died fighting for Charles the First, and John Pascoe Grenville fought the Spanish Armada.

His grandfather on his mother's side and several uncles were army officers campaigning in India. One of them went through the Indian mutiny and the terrible siege of Lucknow. As a little boy, Wilfred was allowed to sit

4

on this uncle's knee and feel the bulge made by a bullet embedded in his forehead.

There were noted scholars as well as noted soldiers in the family. His grandfather Grenfell was house master at Rugby under the great Dr. Arnold. One great-uncle was a distinguished professor at Oxford University. Charles Kingsley, famous as the author of *Westward Ho, Water Babies*, and a number of other books, was a kinsman.

It's a good thing to have such a mingling of explorers, soldiers, and scholars in one's family.

Wilfred was lucky in his birthplace. That village of Parkgate on the Dee was a perfect place to grow up in. A boy had miles of elbow room. Adventure invited him in every direction—down the river to the sea, upstream to the old Roman town of Chester, and across the Dee to the blue hills of Wales. At high tide, a sheet of water spread from the red sandstone wall at Parkgate to the farther shore five miles away. When the tide crept out again, it left behind an expanse of sand never twice the same, cut by small rivulets and set here and there by miniature lakes that mirrored the sky.

Wilfred loved that sandy playground as much as did the birds that circled above it in great flocks. He loved too the salt marshes where the water lost itself in reeds and coarse, rustling grasses.

Mostyn House—the "big house"—would appeal to a boy. It was huge, and old enough to stir his imagination.

There was a roomy nursery and a pleasant walled garden. From the front windows one looked out across the river, and from the back on rolling green fields. It had been a stage-coach inn, "The George," in the long-ago seventeen hundreds, when sailing packets winged their way from the Irish coast to Chester. At its door tired travelers from London had alighted to eat and drink and rest before embarking for Dublin.

Great men had slept under this roof. Here the famous composer, Handel, had cursed the weather. No wonder! For three weeks there wasn't breeze enough to stir the packet's sails, and all that time there lay in Handel's traveling bag the finished score of his great oratorio, *The Messiah*, waiting to be performed for the first time. In the coffee room, Jonathan Swift, author of *Gulliver's Travels*, had smoked and talked.

Steamers took the place of sailing packets. Railroad trains came snorting up the valley to carry passengers to Liverpool and other ports. Gradually the river channel choked up with sand. Parkgate went to sleep. But the ancient inn did not sleep. At Mostyn House, as it was now called, boys lived in a little world of their own presided over by the Grenfells. They ate their meals under the great beams of the old coffee room and played noisy games of cricket and football in the yard where fashionable guests had once strolled.

Wilfred was lucky in the time of his birth. Great Britain was enjoying

A Lucky Boy

"Fifty years of ever-broadening commerce
Fifty years of ever-brightening science
Fifty years of ever-widening Empire."

That is the way Tennyson described the half-century at Queen Victoria's Jubilee in 1887. A boy could grow up during these years with a feeling of security.

What a stimulating time that last half of the nineteenth century was! Men were fighting battles with words instead of guns—in Parliament, on street corners, at dinner tables. They were tremendously excited over electricity, steam engines, balloons, and all sorts of new machines. Charles Darwin had set the world to arguing, sometimes to the point of blows, as to whether "men were descended from monkeys." Herbert Spencer's famous phrase "survival of the fittest" was bandied about wherever men and women gathered.

Reform was in the air. People talked much about the "rights of the common man." Parliament passed a bill reorganizing the army. No longer could a rich man buy a commission for his son. The civil service was reformed. When Wilfred was two years old, the vote was extended to all householders. When he was five, Government schools were established. These were tremendous reforms for nineteenth-century Britain.

This boy was to see surgery completely revolutionized by Sir Joseph Lister's antiseptic methods and by blood tests and X-ray examinations.

7

Indeed it was a wonderful time to be born.

The greatest piece of good fortune that befell this boy has yet to be told. He was born with the gift of turning the business of living into fun—"jolly good fun." What zest for life he did have! The world and all that grew and walked upon it fascinated him. He looked out upon it unafraid. He saw it with an artist's eye for beauty and a scientist's eye for detail. Yes. Young Wilfred Thomason Grenfell certainly got off to a good start.

CHAPTER TWO

So Much to Do

He was the busiest of boys. The days were not long enough for all Wilfred wanted to do. There were not hours enough even in June days when the English twilight lingered till ten o'clock. In the first place, there were his explorations. These covered the sandy shores of the river, the mussel beds where black and white oyster catchers feasted, and the embankment, which had been left unfinished years before on account of quicksands. Sometimes his rovings took him far up into the marshes where the ducks could hide from the sharpest eyes and a boy had to play a long game of hide-and-seek to bring down any of the birds that took refuge in the reeds.

By the time he had reached the great age of eight, young Grenfell was starting out on day-long expeditions all by himself, with a gun over his shoulder and a sandwich in his pocket. What high adventures those solitary trips were! He was Dr. Livingstone in the mysterious, unexplored interior of Africa. Was that a tiger rustling among the reeds? He was Stanley setting out alone to find Livingstone. He was discovering a new continent. Look! The print of men's feet in the sand! Were savages lurking in ambush?

Never would life be more exciting. Often he forgot to eat the sandwich or even to bring it with him. Only the dusk turning the silver water to lead color and warning him that night would soon overtake him made the hunter-explorer conscious of the passing hours.

He liked both the bright blue weather and the steel-gray weather, the days when the wet sand oozing between his bare toes was deliciously cool and the days when the icy ground numbed his toes right through his boots and the wind blowing across the river from the snow-clad hills cut his cheeks like sharp knives.

The business of making "pony money" took a lot of his time. "You boys will have to earn the money yourselves," said Father, when he and Algernon begged for a pony. "The weasels and rats are killing off the chickens. I'll pay threepence for everyone you shoot." The two boys went to work with keen enthusiasm. They spent hours lying in wait around the chicken coops. Every killing was carefully written down in an account book labeled *Pony Money*—"One weasel, threepence. Two rats, sixpence." They caught the fleas that infested the henhouse too. "Three fleas, threepence," the little book recorded.

Hunting for ducks by the river Dee

Earning a pony in this way was slow work. "It will be years before we have enough, even if we save all our allowance money," they decided sorrowfully. After the boys had proved they were willing to work, Father came to their rescue. One morning a beautiful pony appeared in the barn. That was a day! They tried out her gaits in the green fields, along the promenade above the sea wall, and on the sandy shore. Wilfred took wild gallops on that pony. What did it matter if he ended the ride by tumbling over her head or slithering down her tail? Learning to take spills was part of the fun. Still more exciting were races with one of his cousins, who owned a broncho.

"There is *nothing*—absolutely nothing—half so much worth doing as simply messing about in boats." Thus spoke emphatically the Water Rat in *The Wind in the Willows*. This was exactly the way Wilfred felt; and so he was to feel all the rest of his life. To be sure, it was great fun to swim through the cool salt water, diving into whirlpools and drying off on the sun-warmed sands. Those hunting trips in the marshes and those pony races never lost their charm.

Yet this boy would leave off swimming or pony riding or anything else to clamber into a fisherman's boat and go off down the river. Sometimes he would spend a whole day and a night on one of these expeditions, coming home blissfully happy in the early hours of the morning, taking to himself much credit for the silver load in the dory that he had helped to pull out of the sea in the big net.

There was a deserted hut where he liked to stay over night, feeling like Robinson Crusoe. Again, at the invitation of the engine-driver, he would ride on the engine of one of the short trains that occasionally tore the quiet of the valley with their whistles and would take lessons in tending the boiler.

The blue hills on the other side of the river were in a foreign land, so far as Wilfred was concerned. Welshmen, though they lived so near, had strange ways and did not talk like fellow-countrymen, and they lived in towns with tongue-twisting names. Then one day his nurse took him and Algernon for a vacation visit to her home in Wales. People were much alike whether they had unpronounceable names or not, he discovered. At least Welsh boys were just like any others.

There was only one place for a boy to play in this small village, and that was in the public square. The two visitors promptly sought it out. At once a whole gang of rough fellows swooped down upon them, calling names in a strange tongue and pelting them with mud and stones. They weren't going to have these English boys on their playground. Back came the young Grenfells again and again, only to be outnumbered and chased away every time.

"We'll see about this," said Wilfred and Algernon. They went to work gathering deadly ammunition—a large pile of slates which they concealed behind the garden wall of their nurse's cottage. Then, with an air of self-assurance they appeared once more on the green. Again the mob attacked. The strangers retreated fighting as they went, keeping out of reach of the enemy but all the time leading them toward the garden. In a few minutes Wilfred and Algernon were behind the wall and slates were flying over it. Alas for Wilfred's aim! It was too good. One of his slates struck an enemy right over the eye. Blood streamed down the Welsh boy's face. Oh! what had he done? David killed a giant with a sling shot. Had he killed a boy with a slate? He ran to his nurse, sure that he was a murderer.

The injured boy was very much alive and the cut was not deep. As for the Grenfell boys, during the rest of their visit they played on the village green as often as they pleased.

When he was in his early teens, an almost overwhelming desire took possession of Wilfred; he wanted a boat of his own. He just had to have a boat he could sail whenever it suited him to embark. By day and by night he dreamed of paddling a slim, canoe-like craft far up and down the river, penetrating shallow water by-ways and taking rare birds by surprise. How he would race past the fishing boats and laugh at their slow progress. Algernon shared this ambition. So, since there is strength in numbers, the two boys decided to put in a joint request at headquarters.

13

"Father, Wilfred and I want a boat," began older brother.

"Oh yes!" added younger brother fervently, "there isn't anything in the world we want so much."

The would-be skippers were told they could have any kind of craft they desired, that is any they could build themselves.

"We'll get some boards and some nails and—" Wilfred began planning at once.

"Let's see how much allowance money we've got," suggested Algernon.

What counting and recounting of pennies, ha'pennies, shillings, and halfcrowns followed! What excited discussions! They ran down to the sea wall and studied every boat moored there as to shape, size, and probable building costs. Then a visit was paid to the local carpenter's workshop to enlist professional help in the great undertaking.

The next step was to clear the large back room, formerly the boys' nursery, and turn it into a shipyard. Here, directed and helped considerably by the carpenter, they set to work drawing plans, measuring, sawing, and planing. No doubt both boys pictured the result as a thing of beauty that would glide over the Dee with the grace and speed of a racing schooner.

Alas for dreams of a stream-lined craft! When the final hammer blow was struck and the last rough spot planed, the work of their hands stood revealed as a lumbering, box-like affair. Not even the loving builders could call such a tub beautiful. The boys' father was able to think of nothing complimentary to say about this piece of amateur boat-building, so he kept silent, but a cousin had the bad taste to blurt right out that she looked like a coffin. The builders were shocked into action. A coat of bright red paint to offset the funereal lines was the solution. Having applied it, they christened the gay tub the *Reptile,* to suggest sinewy grace. She was launched with pomp and ceremony out of the nursery window onto a sea of green grass.

The *Reptile* carried the two boys on many a voyage. Plain and unromantic-looking though she was, this was an important craft. She was the first of a long series of boats that Wilfred Grenfell was to navigate. Rowing his home-made tub on the Dee was the beginning of an apprenticeship that would make him a Master Mariner and a fearless skipper in heavy seas and on perilous shores.

Next to "messing around in boats," Wilfred's favorite occupation was collecting. The more he explored, the more things he wanted to collect—moths, butterflies, frogs, seaweeds, seashells, flowers, birds, and birds' eggs. He would spend hours stalking waterfowl, counting a day well spent if at the end of it he brought home one new specimen for his collection. By long, careful saving of allowance money, he and Algernon managed to buy a pin-fire, breech-loading gun, their proudest possession—next to the *Reptile*. Armed with this, they would set forth for the haunts of ducks and oyster-catchers and plover and come rowing home, only when forced to by hunger or darkness or a promise made to parents. Keen hunters though they were, they did not shoot down one bird after another just for the fun of seeing how many they could hit. There was a strict code in the Grenfell family about killing birds and beasts. "Never take the life of any living creature except for food, for study, or in self-defense," ran this code, and the boys followed it.

They started a natural history museum of their own. Wilfred turned taxidermist, skinning, stuffing, and mounting the specimens on imitation-rock backgrounds created by himself. Algernon seems to have had more of a bent for carpentering than for the fussier jobs, for he made the wooden cases that held the exhibits. It was a serious business consuming hours of time and carried on with painstaking care.

In the spring and summer months there was simply no rest for Wilfred from the time he got up till he was ordered to bed at night. Added to all the other distractions of the season, were the gorgeous butterflies flying over the sunny fields by day and the pale-tinted moths fluttering in the garden by night. As sure as he was busy with something else, a rare specimen would poise on a flower or go flickering across his path and he would have to get his net and go dashing after it. Stormy days brought no let-up in his affairs. There was still fishing and bird-stalking, and who but a sissy minded getting wet to the skin? If he just had to stay indoors, why then an endless amount of work awaited him—classifying, mounting, and labeling some collection or other.

The Sands of Dee are no nice, safe playground. The tides slide in swiftly turning the wide expanse of sand into a fast-moving stream overtaking the slow and un-wary. There are whirlpools in the river that are like cauldrons filled with boiling, foaming water and there are dangerous quicksands. Charles Kingsley in his poem, *The Sands of Dee*, tells what actually happened to a girl who went across those sands one evening to "call the cattle home."

> "The western tide crept up along the sand,
> And o'er and o'er the sand,
> As far as eye could see.
> The rolling mist came down and hid the land
> And never home came she."

All these perils only made expeditions the more allur-ing to the young explorer. He could swim like a por-poise and was as alert and quick as a brook trout. Treacherous tides and whirling waters held no terrors for him. He knew how to ride them. As for the danger-ous sucking sands, he learned where they were and steered clear of them.

However, like any other boy, he had narrow escapes.

A mishap on his eighth birthday might have ended badly if he had been a panicky child. Wading through shallow water pursuing oyster-catchers, he suddenly plunged headfirst into a deep hole. He promptly kicked himself to the surface and in a few moments had his feet on solid ground again, not particularly frightened and none the worse for the experience except for the loss of the gun he had been carrying and the chilly run home in wet clothes.

The way he could keep his head and get out of difficulties was truly amazing. Still, it's a safe guess that his mother spent anxious hours wondering if Wilfred was all right and that even she sometimes said to the boy's father, "Algernon, do you think we ought to let Wilfred go off by himself so much?"

If the ghosts of the Grenvilles ever came to Parkgate to take a look at their descendants, they must have watched this particular member of the family with delight. One can almost hear old Sir Richard say, "Yon's a fine, brave lad. He'll do."

Meanwhile, without realizing it, this Grenfell boy was fitting himself for the life he was to lead as a man. It was as if an unseen presence were directing him during these years, saying, "Learn to do this—and this—and now this." Of course Wilfred had no idea he was training himself for anything. He only knew that life held all sorts of possibilities for fun, that the days were too short, and that the years had too few days.

Busier and Busier

"Where's the Beast?"

"In the woods, I suppose."

"What's he doing out there in the dark?"

"Oh, he's catching moths."

"Some day he'll get caught himself—sneaking in late for gates."

"Not he! The Beast can look out for himself all right, he can."

The scene of this conversation was a dormitory of Marlborough College. The enormous room—as long and wide as the banquet hall of some old castle—was dark and quiet, save for rustlings and whisperings. There was a boy in each of the twenty-five beds except one—the bed directly under the large window overlooking the garden.

"The Beast" was Wilfred Grenfell, and by all the rules he should have been lying quietly in that empty bed. He was now a fourth form student in an English public school or "college"—what an American boy would call a private "prep" school.

How did he get that ferocious-sounding name? Well, that went back to a fight. Soon after his arrival, a boy began to bully him. He was a big boy, also an "old boy," who had "come up from the lower school." This slim boy, so new and green, was just meant to be picked on, thought he.

Wilfred bristled like a porcupine. "Is that so?" he asked, or something that meant the same thing.

Did he want to fight?

Yes. He did.

The dormitory, the dining hall, the playing field buzzed with excitement.

"But he's bigger than you, and he's done a lot of boxing," warned Wilfred's friends.

"What of it?"

"He'll knock you out before you've had a chance to hit him once."

"You chaps just wait and see."

A crowd gathered to watch the fight. It grew bigger and bigger.

"Look at him! Look at the little beast fight!" they shouted. And that mop of light brown hair waving above his forehead did look a lot like a mane.

Wilfred wasn't big, but was he quick! He knew little about boxing, but how hard those fists could punch! Down went the cocky "old boy."

"Jolly well played, Grenfell! Oh! that was ripping, simply ripping." The boys went wild with excitement. The Beast was absolutely all right.

Now it was the new boy who walked with a swagger.

Marlborough College is in one of the most beautiful spots in England, close to Savenake Forest. This ancient woods was a favorite haunt of Wilfred's. Thrushes and many other birds sang and nested in those moss-hung oaks and by night rare moths flew beneath them. The whisperers in the dormitory that night were right about the boy who should have been lying in the empty bed. He was on the other side of the high wall that enclosed the school grounds, darting about among the trees of the forest. From the dark lantern he carried a beam of light flashed on one great gray trunk after another drawing moths out of the darkness.

"Oh, you beauty!" he exclaimed as a rare specimen alighted obligingly on a twig that had been treated by the collector with a sweet, intoxicating mixture. Then Wilfred danced in and out among the trees from sheer delight over the captured prize, and the mysterious loveliness of the woods on a spring night, and exulted in his stolen freedom from the confining walls of school.

The moth hunt over, then came the most dangerous part of the expedition—getting back to the dormitory unseen. As silent as the moths and owls of the forest, he stole across the grass, climbed the high wall with the ease of a monkey, tiptoed across the laundry roof, and disappeared through a window. A misstep, a sudden noise might have brought serious consequences. To be caught "late for gates"—that is, after the gates had been locked for the night—meant one of the worst consequences a boy like Wilfred could imagine—forced absence from the games he loved to play. However, stalking birds through the marshes of the Dee had taught him to be sure-footed and light-footed. When presently he was in the bed under the garden window, only a few boys were the wiser.

At fourteen, young Grenfell was busier than ever. He was still learning many lessons on his own outside of classrooms. In spite of the rules and restraints necessary in a school of six hundred boys, he managed to venture and explore and to keep on adding to his collections. Fortunately for his happiness, there was a river and a swimming pool here, just outside the school grounds. Of course the allowance of one swim a day was only tantalizing to a boy who had lived in and on the water ever since he could walk. So, like many of the other boys, he counted a stealthy extra swim worth running the risk of being caught and suspended for a week. Thanks to his quick wits, he never was caught.

Wilfred found no difficulty in keeping one rule—that every boy must take part in some form of athletics, unless excused by the school doctor. He loved games, and it was more difficult for his hard-muscled, agile body to be still than not. He learned to box with vim, and played racquets and football. Soon he had earned the right to wear a maroon and white velvet football cap embroidered with the school emblem, an adornment worn only by boys regarded as promising team material.

Wilfred Grenfell also acquired sometime in the course of his education an ability that is rare. Tom Sawyer had it. He could get fun-loving boys to beg, even pay for, the privilege of helping to whitewash a fence as if such work were some new and wonderful game. We find signs of such a budding talent in Wilfred while he was at Marlborough. It seems that whenever a boy was late for tea or dinner, his punishment was to "copy out fifty lines." Punctuality not being one of Wilfred's virtues, he made a point of keeping on hand a reserve supply of the required copy. Yet the reserves were sometimes suddenly exhausted. Then, wonderful to relate, boys less busy with football, boxing, and a number of things than young Grenfell would rally round and do the copying without any reward whatsoever.

How did he persuade them? It's a gift. Perhaps some such conversation as this took place.

Wilfred: It seems a bally shame to miss football practice, but of course it's all my fault.
Other Boy: Why all your fault?
Wilfred: Because I was late for tea yesterday; so I have to do fifty lines.
Other Boy: What beastly luck!

Wilfred: I'll never make the team this way.
Other Boy: Oh I say! Marlborough needs players like you. I'll do that stuff.
Wilfred (simply beaming): That's wonderful, old man. Thanks awfully.

Other boy takes over the copying job with the light of school patriotism in his eyes. Exit Wilfred.

His troubles began when he championed the cause of a boy nicknamed "Mad G." This boy, according to all public school codes of the day, was one to be bullied and ostracized. He was a freak and in American schoolboy language, a "greasy grind." He scorned all games and nearly everything else the average boy cares for. Two things he did love—mathematics and chemistry.

Wilfred recognized this schoolmate as a genius and treated him accordingly. He would listen patiently for hours to the other boy's plans for inventing self-steering torpedoes and flying machines. The two had long talks and worked chemistry problems together as if they were games. To be sure, this bookish chap was queer about football and racquets and no fun except to talk to, but young Grenfell admired him for being himself instead of trying to be something he was not.

"What in the world do you see in that sissy?" the other boys would ask him.

"He's just different from the rest of us, that's all."

"He's different all right, and he'll get over it if he knows what's good for him."

24

"Mad G's got a right to do what he pleases, so long as he doesn't hurt anybody else."

"Oh, has he? We'll see about that."

The Beast was wasting his breath defending his new friend. To be a lone wolf was in itself a crime according to the ideas of these boys. They joined forces against this queer brilliant boy and persecuted him with all the cruelty a group can vent on someone who doesn't fit in.

One day, Wilfred came out of classroom just in time to see a large, sharp-edged lump of coal fly across the hall and hit Mad G. The boy's forehead began to bleed. The fight was on.

"They'll have to fight me too," he said to himself, then hurried the injured boy to the school doctor.

"I fell down," explained G, but the doctor was not fooled and Wilfred had seen all.

"Come on," he suggested, when they were back in the classroom. "Let's move your desk over into my corner." There and then he took G under his personal protection and stood ready at all times to defend him with a pair of hard fists.

It was war all right—a particularly baffling kind of war. A mob "ganged up" on Wilfred, determined to get him by foul means rather than fair fight. They lay in wait for him on stairways and in dark halls. He couldn't fight the whole gang, so had to beat them in a game of wits. They would expect him to go this way; so he would go that way. They had dodged behind one door; he would slip in through another. Thus his life went for months.

The swimming race held about this time was a bitter experience. Wilfred was sure he could win after all the swimming he had done. Yet how long that tank did seem! Could he make it? Now he was ahead. No. Jones had caught up with him. He mustn't let him get ahead. "Come on, old man! Come on!" yelled the onlookers, almost tumbling into the water in their excitement. Suddenly Wilfred realized that this rooting was not for him. It was for the other chap. Of course his own friends were cheering him on, but their voices were drowned out by the roars for Jones.

Well, he'd win now if it killed him. And win he did. Yet there was little joy in that victory.

Yes. He lost many friends, and this was hard on The Beast after all that popularity. Yet "friends" like those were really small loss. He had gained the courage to take an unpopular stand, and he would need a store of that courage later on.

How was this boy, so busy with his own education, finding time for class work? Well, apparently his mind was as quick as his swift-running, fast-dodging body. He reports that "work came easy to him" and that he won a scholarship during his first term at Marlborough. Anything to be memorized was learned from a loose page pulled out of his pocket at odd moments when he had to be indoors anyway—between courses at dinner or during chapel. Mathematics and chemistry, his favorite subjects, were more play than work, but languages ancient and modern were drudgery for him.

On the whole, the time spent at Marlborough was not an especially delightful period. Looking back in later years, Grenfell thinks of those days as a time when "one's bristles were generally up." Probably a less independent boy with fewer interests of his own would have been more content in a school of six hundred boys.

One of the pleasantest places in the whole school was the sickroom, presided over by fatherly Dr. Fergus. "Old Fungi," the boys called him, not in ridicule but in warm affection.

"I don't like the way that cough hangs on, Grenfell," he told Wilfred one day during his second year at Marlborough, after the boy had been in his care for several weeks. Murmuring something about "congestion of the lungs" he prescribed so delightful a cure the patient could not believe he had heard aright.

"Beg pardon, sir?"

"I said you must go to a warm climate and just live out of doors all winter."

Old Fungi ran no risks, and there were no X-ray machines in those days to take the guess-work out of his diagnosis.

"Oh, really, sir?" He tried not to sound too pleased but succeeded badly.

What luck! What absolutely ripping, unbelievable luck! It was worth the price of a cough. It would have been almost worth an attack of smallpox to "just live out of doors" the rest of the winter.

A letter was dispatched to Mr. Grenfell. From Mostyn House, a letter promptly went to Hyères on the French Riviera, addressed to an aunt of Wilfred's. "Send him right along," she wrote back. So Wilfred was packed off to a villa on the shores of the Mediterranean Sea.

There followed bliss—undiluted, undisturbed bliss—such as no one can expect more than once or twice in a whole life-time. Here, under warm, sunny skies in one of the fairest spots in the world, he roamed at will on foot and on horseback. He bathed as many times a day as he liked in that bluest of seas, fairly living in it and on the white beach. The flowery hillsides behind the villa were a butterfly paradise, also paradise for a butterfly collector. There were two lively girl cousins for company. His "congestion of the lungs" did not seem to prevent his leading an extremely active life with them.

Sometimes, on high days, the whole household just went a-pleasuring. The Carnival at Nice was such a day, when the city was given over to masqueraders, flowers, parades, pranks, and laughter. A trip to the gardens of La Mortola across the border in Italy was another high day—a series of colorful pictures. The whole visit at his aunt's villa seemed a glimpse of heaven and was one of the memories of his boyhood that he would always treasure.

Wilfred carried on all sorts of studies and investigations of his own there on the shores of the Mediterranean. That questioning mind of his was continually suggesting, "Let's go and see what that bird is," or "Isn't this a new kind of butterfly? Why not catch it?" or "You really should take home some of these shells." Collecting could now be pursued at any time, unhampered by rules or locked gates.

Possibly he learned as much during these weeks of freedom as he would have in school. In spite of his dislike for languages, he was soon talking French with some ease, through the necessity of making himself understood in a French community. Learning a language in this way seemed comparatively painless. Zoology as taught by himself to himself was fascinating. He penned up frogs in little tanks of water provided with small ladders and carefully observed the captives, noticing how they always climbed up the ladders when wet weather was approaching. In the same first-hand manner, he studied trap-door spiders and he bred beautiful butterflies and moths.

This blissful state was too good to last. Presently a letter from home announced that a boy who could do all the things Wilfred wrote about in his letters was certainly well enough to do some studying. An English tutor was engaged to put the boy to work. How like a serpent in the Garden of Eden this well-meaning man seemed!

Yet life was still pleasant here. Mathematics was as much fun as ever, and Wilfred liked part of the French lessons—learning the fables of La Fontaine by heart. Then the lizards that slithered up and down the walls of the tutor's villa brightened study hours considerably. It was sport to watch them catch flies and to flip one of them off the wall with a switch before it did a vanishing act or fooled him by shedding its tail. There was time for horseback rides on the beach, for swims, and for the pursuit of happiness and knowledge after his own fashion. And he was still in that earthly paradise.

Going back to Marlborough College the following summer, to grayer skies than those the Mediterranean mirrored even in winter, to routine and fixed hours and places for doing things was like returning to prison after a parole. However, Wilfred's stay this time was comparatively short. His father, realizing that this boy of his with a talent for educating himself made faster progress outside of school walls than within them, arranged for a tutor to complete his son's preparation for taking the final examinations.

Two years later, a most disturbing question was put to Wilfred.

CHAPTER FOUR

A Disturbing Question

"What are you going to do in life?"

"Do, Father?"

"Yes. What comes next for you?"

"Well, I'd like to go tiger-hunting in India."

The tiger skins and elephant tusks and deer heads in Mostyn House had always fascinated Wilfred. Again and again he had dreamed of exploring in tropical jungles on elephant back. What magnificent man-eating tigers, what royal lions he had brought down in imagination!

"I mean what profession are you going to fit yourself for? How do you want to make your living?"

"Oh-h-h! I hadn't thought about that."

At eighteen, Wilfred was ready for the next step, even if he did not know what it was to be. Preparatory school work was done, and he had learned all he could along and upon the Dee. The fishermen had taught him what they knew about the tides, the weather, and fishing. He had learned about engines from the men who drove the railroad locomotives up and down the valley. The creatures of the marshes had tutored him in alertness and patience. He could build a boat—after a fashion —and manage it in foul weather as well as fine, against head winds and fair winds. His muscles were hard, his body was lithe and responded quickly to the directions his keen mind gave it. He could swim, box, play football, hold his own in a fight, and win the respect of other boys.

Yet of one aspect of life this boy was wholly ignorant. Just as the cold winds were shut away from the roses and jasmine in the walled garden of Mostyn House, so the world of fierce struggle had been shut away from him by the loving care of his parents and by the seclusion of Parkgate. He scarcely knew that poverty existed. The fishermen along the river lived comfortably, though simply. To be sure there were some old ladies who used to come once a week in winter time to the Grenfell kitchen for a square meal and buckets of soup to carry home with them, but theirs was a genteel sort of poverty, and anyway Wilfred seldom saw them.

Now this question his father had asked brought him up short. How much he had been taking for granted all these years! Money didn't just flow from some inexhaustible source. He would have to learn to do something for which someone would pay him. It was an almost overwhelming thought. Like many another eighteen-year-old, he hadn't the remotest idea what he wanted to do.

A much-traveled lady was consulted. She was the mother of one of Wilfred's best friends and supposedly possessed more knowledge of the world than the Grenfell elders. Yet she was of no help at all—except perhaps as a bubble-pricker. Again the boy couldn't resist bringing up the subject of explorations in India, only to be told that a young man couldn't possibly support himself by exploring jungles and hunting tigers. There could be little question about the truth of her statement, since she had lived in India for many years. Her advice was that he become a clergyman.

"There have always been clergymen in your family," she reminded him.

Wilfred tried hard to see himself in the place of the local rector. It was utterly impossible. "I don't want to wear different clothes from other people. I couldn't, simply couldn't, be on my dignity all the time," he told her.

No pedestals or pulpits for him! He liked the give and take with plain people that a chap could have only by putting himself on their level. Suppose the fishermen on the Dee should be suddenly awed and tongue-tied, when he came around. How terrible that would be! He wanted vigorous action of some sort in his lifework too, much more than an English parson had. If only he could just buy a boat and earn his living fishing.

So the lady counselor left him exactly where he was
—in a state of confusion.

There was in Parkgate a plain man with a great deal
of good sense, who was often called upon to give advice.
He was the friend of all boys, and he had known Wilfred Grenfell ever since he was born. This man was the
family doctor. At his father's suggestion, Wilfred went
and had a quiet talk with him.

"So you haven't the ghost of an idea what you want
to do next?"

"No, sir." By this time the boy had given up talking
about India and tiger-hunting.

The doctor was silent for a few moments. He liked
Wilfred—that straight, level glance of his, the independent way he held his shoulders and walked, those hard-
hitting, fast-hitting fists, the mixture of seriousness and
fun in him. How he threw himself into everything he
did! On the playing field in front of Mostyn House, he
ran with a football as if nothing else in life mattered.
Out hunting in the marshes, the doctor had seen him
waiting, waiting, motionless as a stone for hours in a
pouring rain to bring down some rare bird. And what a
streak of lightning he was in the fields with that butterfly net! If the boy could only harness that enthusiasm
and hitch the traces to some big piece of work, what
wouldn't he accomplish? Was he cut out for a doctor?
Perhaps between them they could find out.

"What studies did you like best in school?"

"I was keen about chemistry and mathematics, sir."

A Disturbing Question

After a few more questions, the doctor started in talking rather casually about his own work—what he might have to do in the course of a day. Yesterday a call had come from Chester. The mother of a large family had fallen and broken her leg, but she'd be around almost as good as new in a few weeks. Today a small boy down the river had been choking for each breath with croup, but he was fine now. He stole a quick glance at Wilfred. Fires were kindling in those gray-blue eyes and he was sitting forward in his chair. The doctor went on talking.

The boy's thoughts ran somewhat like this—Why this ordinary man, who spent his days driving a span of horses over the country roads, measuring pills and potions, bandaging and poulticing, he was like a magician when you stopped to think about it. He put splintered bones together and made them whole. He could quicken a heart that had almost stopped beating. A few minutes difference in the time his fast horses took to reach a house might mean the difference between life and death for somebody. What power was his!

On a shelf in the doctor's office stood a large bottle. Inside it was a queer-looking gray mass, like a large and rather shapeless pickle. Wilfred had never particularly noticed this exhibit before. Today the doctor took it down and let his visitor examine it closely. The gray mass was a human brain. Everything the body did was directed by this organ. From it messages went out to nerves and muscles with the speed of lightning.

Now Wilfred was listening to what the doctor said

35

as if he couldn't bear to miss a single word. The brain had a telegraph system as perfect as any Morse code. This body of his was even more wonderful than those steam engines he had helped to stoke on railroad trains. It beat all the new machines people talked about so much nowadays. In a million years nobody could invent any machine half so marvelous. He had found it—the answer to that disturbing question. He knew now exactly how he wanted to earn his living.

What did Wilfred's father say when his son came running home, with a light of discovery in his eyes and announced, "I'm going to be a doctor." Well, he certainly must have been enormously relieved. This boy of his had settled at last on something he really wanted to do. He had chosen a profession. Moreover, the decision fitted in well with the father's own plans, for he had decided to lease the school at Parkgate and accept the offer he had received of a chaplaincy in the great London Hospital.

The next step for Wilfred was to set to work cramming for examinations—ten of them. Before he could enter the University of London, before he could take courses at London Hospital, these examinations must be passed. This sounds like hard work ahead. Yet it seems to have been accomplished without too great difficulty. That enthusiasm of his helped him through the ordeal. It made him see obstacles as if through the small end of an opera glass.

They lay in wait for him

A Disturbing Question

The old house on the Dee became a scene of bustle and confusion. The place was astir with unwonted activities from top to bottom. Early and late, footfalls were heard on the stairs. Through all the daylight hours, the hammering of boxes and the rumbling of trunks being moved about were a solemn accompaniment to family life. The Grenfells were packing up, and Mostyn House had been the family home for too many years to be left easily.

One can imagine Wilfred making many goodby visits —to the fishermen, to the engineers on the railroad trains, and to the doctor, who must have had much parting advice to give. There were last expeditions to be made— up and down the river, and to the marshes, and of course he couldn't resist trying to bring down one more bird and catch a few more butterflies for those collections. Packing up his belongings was a miserable business. He had to leave behind the stuffed birds and his moths and all sorts of mementoes and curios that he wanted to take to London. Unfortunately, there was a limit to the amount of luggage that could be piled on the vans.

When the heavy old front door of Mostyn House shut behind the eighteen-year-old boy in 1883, it closed on a period of his life. He may not have realized that those carefree days of wandering along the Dee were over. Yet they were. To be sure, he would come back to this childhood home on vacations for many years. It would still be in the family, since Algernon, who was now in Oxford, planned to take over the management of the school. The cases of stuffed birds and butterflies would still be there.

Yet Mostyn House would not be Wilfred's home again in the sense it was home now. He would feel a little like a visitor when he came back. And he would come not as a boy, but as a man, who had lived in one of the most sordid city slums in the whole world, a man with work to do. In a sense, however, the sands of Dee were always to be Wilfred Grenfell's home. So long as he lived he would draw strength from memories of life there, and from visits to the old house as a tree draws nourishment from unseen places with one deep tap-root.

Just now he was looking forward not backward. Tremendous changes were in store for him, and he welcomed them. The desire to venture greatly was strong within him. He was eager to see the hospital where he would be a medical student—the largest hospital in the British Isles. What would life be like in that huge gray building and at the University? Would he be on the football team? Would he row in University boat races? Anyway he would learn fascinating things, things that only doctors know. What an experience it was going to be! So, with the same zest for life he had shown ever since he first began getting about on his two sturdy legs, Wilfred left the sleepy town where he was born and set forth with his family for London.

CHAPTER FIVE

So This Is London!

"Look at us! We're supposed to be homes," cried out the mean little houses and the dreary tenements.

"Get out of the way or be knocked down. Life is cheap here," warned the hoofs of the dray horses as they clattered on the cobble stones.

"Life is a battle," was written on the tense, lined faces of the men and women.

The young man from Parkgate now lived and worked in the teeming East End of London. He was rubbing elbows with people such as he had never met before except in books and newspapers. Pickpockets hung about the streets at all hours, lifting pocketbooks and watches from the unwary. Burglars plied their trade by night, as thick as prowling cats. Evil intent was in their leering glances.

More depressing than these hardened men were the children of the streets. Could this little chap with his wise old face really be a child? How fast he took to his heels at the sight of a policeman! He had probably grabbed that apple he was eating from a fruit stall. Was that a little girl hurrying by or a dwarfed old woman? Her slender shoulders drooped, pulled over by the weight of the baby she carried. And she looked as if she hadn't eaten a square meal in weeks.

"Poverty" was no longer just a word to Wilfred Grenfell. He saw honest, hard-working people going round and round a tread-mill without hope of anything more than enough food to keep them alive and a dark, stuffy hole to sleep in. The rats of Parkgate fared better than did some of these men and women. No wonder many of them seemed like mere animals. The old women picking up the droppings from vegetable carts and digging about in garbage pails—could they be human beings? They were more like stray dogs. And those bleary-eyed, swollen-faced men that came reeling out of Whitechapel saloons, were they actually of the same breed as the clear-eyed, kindly fishermen on the Dee? Wrecked ships Wilfred had seen before, but shipwrecked men such as the slums of London held were a new experience.

The great soot-blackened pile of stone that was the London Hospital could accommodate nearly a thousand patients, and it was always full. Within those walls, the young medical student—when he reached the stage of "walking the hospital"—saw more misery than he had supposed existed on the whole planet. There were pa-

tients so desperate they had to be watched every minute
lest they end their own lives. Some of them were nursed
back to health only to shoot themselves or to be brought
to trial for a crime and hanged.

To be pulled up from a sleepy fishing village and
transplanted to these streets was a shock—a sobering experience. Even the Grenfell home was burglarized—
twice. One of these breaks was in broad daylight. It was
typical of Wilfred's fearlessness, also his inexperience,
that he—the only member of the family at home—chased
the robbers out of the house and over a high fence.
Lucky indeed for him, that he did not succeed in catching up with them.

Of course that well-developed sense of humor of his
stood the young man from Parkgate in good stead.
There was frequent cause for chuckles and laughter
here, as well as for pity and dismay. Some of the back-
talk of the hospital patients was side-splitting. He never
forgot the drunken woman who explained the ghastly
scalp wounds he dressed by saying, "Sure me and another loidy was just havin' a few words."

Then too, as we saw at Marlborough, young Grenfell could look through people's outside shells and un-
cover the fineness that often lay underneath the rough
layers. A Norwegian sailor was one rare spirit the medical student long remembered. He was operated on at the
hospital by the chief surgeon, Sir Frederick Treves, and
discharged as cured. Three weeks later back he came

and asked to see the man who had performed the operation. When Sir Frederick appeared, the sailor proceeded to cut out of the lining of his coat the five-kronen
gold piece sewn into it for emergencies and presented it
to the great man. Apologizing for the delay in expressing his thanks, he explained that for those three weeks he
had been wandering around with no money trying to
find another berth on a ship. Now he had just secured
one and dared part with the gold piece. To go hungry
for the sake of paying a doctor who has presented no bill
—that is a kind of integrity rare indeed in this world!

Leisure hours, as usual, were packed full of activities.
Games appealed to Wilfred as much as ever. He rowed
in the inter-hospital rowing race, played in the inter-
hospital football games, and for two years won second
place for hammer-throwing in the united hospital sports.
He found time to be secretary to the cricket, football,
and rowing clubs of London University in successive
years. During his one term at Oxford, he distinguished
himself on the football team there.

Best of all were those summer vacations! What a joy
to leave the heat, the dirt, the sights and sounds of city
slums! Again he was "messing around in boats" with his
brother, Algernon. Now, instead of the *Reptile*—which
had long since gone to the bottom of the Dee—they
cruised in an old fishing smack hired for these occasions.
Gleefully changing its name from the *Oyster* to the
Roysterer, they embarked on real voyages upon the Irish

Sea, sailing wherever the wind would take them and living for the most part on what the sea and the woods supplied in the way of fish and game. The duties of skipper, mate, and cook were shared by the two brothers. For the jobs of second mate and deckhand on these happy-go-lucky trips, there were always plenty of volunteers. A little rowing, a little swimming, now and then a mountain climb or a visit to some old ruined castle, fishing, hunting, and games filled the days up to the last minute of daylight.

During the years at the London Hospital and in the University, the boy, who had wanted to make a career of tiger-hunting, grew up. In such surroundings, no one could take happiness and security for granted. He had learned the value of money too—from seeing what extreme poverty could do to people. Then, before student years were over, Wilfred's family life was greatly changed. That wise and gentle father died. Mrs. Grenfell moved to the suburbs.

Independent he had always been, but until now he was conscious at all times of the comforting security that a happy home gives one, like the glow of an ever-burning fire. Now there was a great gap in the family circle. Of course he saw his mother often and talked things over with her. Yet he was on his own as he had never been before—living in his own "diggings."

He was independent in another sense. A young man enrolled at the University and the Hospital had com-

plete freedom to make something of himself or go to the
devil. Whether he got the training he needed to become
a doctor was entirely his own affair. The lectures were
there; he could take them, or he could leave them and
dissipate and there was every opportunity to do the lat-
ter. A record for perfect attendance was merely a matter of tipping the beadle who called the roll. Examinations were the only check on what the student did with
his time—the great days of reckoning.

That self-reliance developed by Grenfell, the boy,
stood Grenfell, the student, in good stead. His enthusiasm helped too. The things he learned at lectures, the
discoveries he made at home with his own microscope,
the patients—both as cases and as human beings—the life
in the East End streets—all these things interested him
keenly. Just as those days on the Dee, at Marlborough
College, and in southern France had been far too short,
so now there was not time enough for all he wanted to
do in London. Life would always be like that for Wilfred Grenfell.

A Light in a Tent

"Hello! What's going on in there? A circus?" Wilfred asked himself. It was evening. He was on his way home from visiting an out-patient case and had come upon a large tent pitched in a vacant lot. A light streamed from the entrance. Shadow pictures of people were thrown in sharp relief against the white cloth. Sounds of singing and speaking floated into the street. There was certainly a crowd inside. "I'll just pop in and see what it's all about," he decided.

Grenfell was still exploring and investigating. In London he liked to prowl around the streets studying the ways of men. What a variegated pattern of street life there was! It fascinated him—the sidewalk markets where almost anything could be bought from a three-legged cripple of a bed to a rusty birdcage or a second-hand suit of clothes, the soapbox debaters in Victoria Park, the boys and girls dancing to a tune played on a barrel organ, the costers, the beggars, the brawlers.

"Pretty dull!" was his verdict on the meeting a few minutes later. That old chap making a prayer was just one of those bores who are forever getting up and talking in public. Probably it was the first chance he'd ever had to get so many people to listen to him. The prayer droned on and on. The young man started for the entrance. As he wove in and out among the men, women and children that filled the aisle, a stocky, bearded man rose from his seat on the platform. "Let us sing a hymn," he announced, "while our brother is finishing his prayer."

Good for the man with the beard. He did seem to know how to handle a meeting. Looked like a real person too, with some fun in him. An American, evidently. The young investigator decided to stay, and see what came next. Anyway it would be amusing to listen to him. Americans had such funny accents.

When both hymn and prayer were ended, the leader began to speak. He talked simply without any ranting or fireworks. Yet his earnestness held the crowd silent, intent, almost as if he had reached out a hand and touched each one. At least that is the way Grenfell felt.

"Who is he? Who *is* that man?" he wanted to know as soon as the meeting was over.

"The preacher? 'E's that h'American h'evangelist folks is making so much talk about. Moody, that's 'is nime," was the reply in the very best Cockney.

So the stout man with the beard was Dwight L. Moody, the famous American preacher. Wilfred had never supposed that a popular evangelist who held meetings in tents would be like this man—so quiet, so simple. Out in the noisy street, that compelling voice was still in his ears.

Follow me, and I will make you fishers of men. Fishers of men and helpers of men were needed here and now just as much as they were in Galilee nearly two thousand years ago. Why hadn't he ever thought about that before?

"Who yer think yer are—the Prince of Wales? Taking up the whole sidewalk like that?"

"Sorry," apologized Grenfell to the man he had jostled. He could not have told whether he was on the sidewalk or on the cobblestones of the street. There was a far-away look in his eyes. What was it the American had said?

If God gives you a meal in the morning, He expects it to make you fit to give someone else something in the evening.

"Watch yer step there, young feller!"

"Beg pardon!"

No, he certainly wasn't watching his step as he walked home that night. Words that the preacher had spoken were repeating themselves over and over in his mind and he was thinking—thinking hard.

"Religion's not just something you believe," he said to himself. "A chap has to do something about it—put it into action." Either you lived it from day to day and expressed it in your work and in all your dealings with others, or else—well, what did any other kind of religion amount to?

Important events often seem casual enough at the time. To stray by chance into an East London tent meeting, to remain listening to a stranger out of curiosity—this would not seem like the setting for any great change in Wilfred Grenfell's life. Yet it was. Two years earlier, a talk with a country doctor had sent him home declaring, "I want to be a doctor." Tonight, after listening to Mr. Moody, he was still determined to be a doctor, and also to follow the example set by one known as the Great Physician.

He had been like a boat without a compass. Now he had something to steer by.

All of a sudden he felt personally responsible for a whole lot of things that before hadn't seemed his business at all. The little street toughs, for instance, with their old, worldly-wise faces. Those boys hadn't a chance of growing into anything but bums and criminals. How had he been able to live here for two years without trying to do something for them? Why, they wanted exactly the same things he had had on the Dee and at school. They ought to be swimming, rowing boats, boxing, playing games.

"All your life, Wilfred Grenfell, you've been having a wonderful time," he told himself. "Now, how about going shares with some of these chaps who've been cheated out of just about everything that makes life any fun at all?"

This is exactly what he proceeded to do.

"Over we go!"

"Hey, Jimmy, you're tearing your britches."

"Give me a leg up, old man, will you?"

"First man over the fence gets the first swim."

The scene was the entrance to Victoria Park. The time was early morning before the tall iron gates had been unlocked for the day. Those present were a bunch of highly assorted boys and a man of about twenty. The goal of this little band of early risers was the lake within the Park. They were hurrying to get a swim before those all-too-popular waters had been muddied by many bathers. The young man scrambling over the gate with the boys and presently giving them a swimming lesson was, of course, Wilfred Grenfell.

This class was only one of the many ways he had discovered to share the pleasant things of life that had been his with the boys in this crowded city, who had almost no chance for good times and every chance to get into scrapes, into run-ins with the police, and even into jail. Now on Saturday nights, he would clear the dining-room of the house where he lived and turn it into a gymnasium. Here he gave boxing lessons and taught boys to swing clubs and perform on parallel bars. In the back yard noisy and fiercely contested quoit-pitching matches were held.

He joined a fellow medical student in holding a Sunday school class for a group of boys in one of the toughest sections of East London. All the muscle acquired in football games and rowing matches was needed to handle them. Those boys were as wild as wolf cubs. They would steal anything and everything in the schoolroom that wasn't nailed down and break every breakable object, unless they were watched constantly. If chucked out of the class for bad behavior, a boy would just wait for his chance to have sweet revenge. One trouble-maker, whom Grenfell had taken by the collar and pitched out into the street, lay in ambush for his teacher after class in a dark alley and showered him with mud and stones. Such experiences did not discourage Wilfred at all. We find him, as time went on, having more rather than less to do with his young neighbors.

"Is the water up there blue like in pictures or all dirty like the river here?"

"It's blue like the sky? Sa-ay that must look pretty."

"Was the bloke what lived in that castle where you went a real duke or was yer kidding us?"

"Wot's it feel like to be on top of a mountain? Does it make a chap dizzy?"

The questions came thick and fast from the group of boys crowded around Wilfred Grenfell. Back from a vacation "roystering" on the Irish Sea, brown as an

African native, he was sharing the experience with them. At least he thought he was sharing it. With what gusto he told of flying along in his boat under full sail as if riding a great bird, of pulling silver fish out of the sea, of diving off the side for a cool before-breakfast dip.

Then came these questions.

What kind of sharing was this—telling about sailing and fishing and mountain climbing to boys who had never seen a mountain, never felt salt spray on their cheeks, who half doubted if the sea were blue! To look into their wondering faces made him feel guilty. Why this was downright cruel of him!

"If you had to spend the whole summer here in the heat and the noise and dirt, how would *you* like to hear all about someone else's fun on a sailing trip?" he asked himself.

"I never saw it that way before."

"Well, what are you going to do now?"

It did not take Grenfell long to decide what he would do. These boys were going along with him next time— at least as many of them as could be packed into a boat without sinking her. They thought he was "just kidding" when he told them so. But go next summer they did, thirteen strong.

Now began yearly camping trips for East London boys somewhat like the expeditions Boy Scouts make today. The equipment (furnished by the leader or by friends of his) was simple—uniforms consisting of blue

51

knickers and gray flannel shirts and long burlap bags filled with hay for beds. A few tents and some decrepit old boats made up the rest of the camping outfit. Rules were few but strictly enforced.

Were these vacations popular? Judge for yourself. Beginning with thirteen boys, the band increased to thirty the second year and then reached nearly one hundred the third summer. No doubt plenty more young East-enders would have jumped at the chance to go, if tents and boats had only been stretchable.

Grenfell showed good sense in the way he conducted these trips. In a day when people were inclined to do things for the poor in a patronizing spirit, he took care not to rob his campers and their parents of their independence and self-respect. Every boy was encouraged to save up to pay as much as he could of his expenses, which were kept at the lowest possible figure, and of course each camper had to do his share of the work.

What days those were for city prisoners! They swam, played water polo, rowed boats, climbed mountains, slept in tents, pulled fish out of the sea—in short did the things that any boy just longs to be doing when days are long, when fields are green, and the sandy shores of the sea lie warm under a summer sun.

It's quite possible that the one who had the most fun out of those vacations was Wilfred Grenfell. To be sure, his patience was tried again and again by boys who went wild in their new-found freedom and by boys who

Over Victoria Park fence

didn't know the meaning of the word "sportsmanship."
Yet that sense of humor of his was equal to the situation.
It worked overtime beginning on the morning set for
the start, when an old costermonger drove up to his
door. This volunteer truckman was the proud father of
one of the campers. His horse, bought cheap because
she "had something the matter with her legs," and
hitched to an ancient, rattling cart, was a comic sight.
Off she hobbled to the railway station with the dunnage.
Off went a shouting bunch of boys, fairly delirious with
joy. From this merry departure on, the boys' comments
on the sights they saw and the people they met kept
their leader laughing. Even their worst deviltry usually
had an excruciatingly funny side.

Through the eyes of these new companions, the
young medical student saw accustomed things afresh,
as if never really seen before, not only the fields and
mountains and the sea, but also customs, conventions,
and social classes. From them he learned of the kinship
that exists between people just as human creatures, regardless of birth or race or education. For years he
would keep in touch with some of these campers, and
never so long as he lived would he forget adventures and
misadventures shared with them by land and by sea.

CHAPTER SEVEN

"Where Is the Ship?"

Cold rain beat against the windows of the Yarmouth-bound train, obscuring the little that could be seen outside in the dusk. One of the passengers on this winter's night kept peering through the dripping panes, as if it were hard for him to wait for the trip to be over. He was a slim, muscular young man of about medium height, with light brown hair and a brown mustache. His gray-blue eyes could be twinkling one minute and be looking extremely serious the next. Tonight they were serious, with an expectant gleam in them. The impatient traveler was Wilfred Grenfell, and he was eager to see a certain ship that lay anchored at a quay in Great Yarmouth.

Pictures of that craft had filled his thoughts for months. "Soon I'll be setting out on a boat like that," he had thought whenever his work had taken him near the East London docks, where the stately, tall-masted ships known as Indiamen were being loaded and unloaded.

54

The nearer the date set for the voyage had approached, the harder was it for him to wait. Now the day had come. Tonight he was going aboard the ship. His imagination raced out there ahead of the engine. It had reached the quay.

This was the same adventuring, explorative Wilfred who four years ago had longed to ship to India and go tiger-hunting—yet a different Wilfred. He was Dr. Grenfell, a member of the College of Physicians and Surgeons and of the Royal College of Surgeons of England. Since receiving his degree, he had been House Surgeon at the London Hospital. Now he was off to combine work and service to others with a long cruise.

"Grenfell, how would you like to go for a while to the North Sea and look after the men in the fishing fleet?" Sir Frederick Treves, Grenfell's chief at the London Hospital, had asked him a few months earlier.

"That sounds like just the kind of berth I *would* like, Sir Frederick," had been the prompt answer. "To get away from all this—a big hospital, a big city, noise, crowds—that appeals to me right now, for a while anyway. It would seem like a vacation."

Wilfred Grenfell, as we have seen, was lucky in his ancestors and his parents. Another piece of good luck was in having so great a surgeon and so wise a human being for his friend and adviser as was this man. Had it not been for Sir Frederick Treves, he might never have seen the Labrador coast or have been a doctor to fishermen. There would have been adventure in his life—that is certain. He was not cut out for a humdrum routine or for a career that was merely money-earning. Yet he would have followed some quite different path to find adventure.

Sir Frederick, like this pupil of his, was never so happy as when he was "messing about in boats." He had cruised in the North Sea and visited the fishing fleets and knew well what desperate need for a doctor there was among the men and boys who practically lived their lives afloat off "the banks." He knew Wilfred Grenfell too. This young man stood out among all the medical students who had walked the hospital since he had been Head Surgeon. What a gift he had for swift, accurate diagnosis! How keenly interested he was in every patient both as a case and as a human being! Adventure on land and sea he loved, but especially adventure on sea. There was any amount of fun in him. Yet he took life with great seriousness too. He firmly believed that his talents, his training, his health—all had been given him that he might help others. Sir Frederick Treves understood this philosophy of life, for it happened to be his own. He had even been a silent partner in some of those camping trips Grenfell had conducted.

There was, it seemed, a mission ship that made regular trips to the fishing grounds, giving first aid to injured men and holding religious services. The Royal National Mission to Deep Sea Fishermen, which was in charge of this work, now wished to add to its staff a muscular young doctor who didn't mind roughing it, and Sir Frederick, as a member of their council, was trying to find such a doctor.

A muscular young doctor who didn't mind roughing it! The young man recognized a description of himself when he heard one. To live at sea and doctor real fishermen! Hadn't he grown up with men who lived by casting lines and hauling nets? Hadn't he liked better than any boy's play to go down the Dee with them and take an oar or lend a hand with the nets? And these men needed his help, desperately. He would go—any time, right away.

"Wait till January," advised the older man. "You're seaman enough to like a bit of weather and the sight of white teeth in the waves. Summer's the time when the old ladies go up there for a rest."

So Grenfell had waited.

Now, after all those months, the North Sea voyage was about to begin. Already the train whistle shrieked a warning that it was near Great Yarmouth. It was beginning to slow down for the station. At almost the same instant as the engine came to a stop, Grenfell leaped to the platform with his bags. The ugly, dimly-lighted station seemed hardly the setting for the start of an adventure. Nor was the stout, blue-uniformed fisherman who waited there a swash-buckling figure. The dilapidated cab in which the two of them set out for the docks, the

57

spiritless horse harnessed to the cab, the drizzling rain—
these things gave the traveler all at once a feeling that he
was about to embark on a forlorn, joyless enterprise.

As the horse went clop-clopping slowly along a dark
road, Grenfell's spirits, that had been rising steadily for
weeks, began to drop precipitately. The man in the blue
uniform seemed to be taking him to the last jumping off
place on the earth. Clop! Clop! Clop! The hoof beats
were a slow, heavily-accented accompaniment to his own
thoughts.

Quite suddenly the driver said, "Whoa," and pulled
on the reins.

"Is this the quay?" asked Grenfell doubtfully. He had
alighted from the cab and was straining his eyes in a vain
attempt to see tall spars against the sky.

"Ay."

"But where's the ship?" he demanded. Had some
practical joke, some trick, been played upon him? There
was no sign of hull or spars.

"Right down there, sir," the fisherman pointed to
what looked like two stubby posts. "Those are her masts.
It's low tide," he added, as if that were sufficient explanation for the hull not being visible.

The young man walked to the edge of the water and
looked down into the gloom below for convincing evi-
dence that a boat really was docked there. If his spirits
had been low at the railroad station, they had dropped
to zero by this time. The craft he could just make out

bobbing up and down with the tide was scarcely larger than the *Roysterer*. Compared with an East Indiaman, it was no more than a tub.

Well, the cab was still there and his bags were still in it. He'd turn around and go back, even if he had to wait all night in that dark hole of a station for a train to London. Yet it was not so easy to give up a plan upon which he had set such store. And, after all, Sir Frederick had seen this boat. It must be seaworthy, and perhaps it was bigger than it looked in the dark. As he wavered, a voice called up out of the moist darkness from the deck of that tub. The sound of it seemed to change at once the complexion of the voyage from a doubtful venture to a reasonable undertaking. There are voices like that.

Grabbing a rope Grenfell slid down. Unfortunately the rigging had just been thoroughly greased and tarred. His clothes and his dignity both suffered from the experience, and, in spite of his seagoing vacations, the new ship's doctor must have impressed the crew that night as a complete land-lubber.

Small though the boat was, it was decidedly shipshape. The decks were spotless. So was the white suit of the cook and steward. Living quarters were cramped but neat as a pin. The whole atmosphere was so friendly and reassuring that Wilfred Grenfell forgot all about East Indiamen. By the time anchor was hoisted and the boat was headed for the North Sea, he was thanking his stars that he was aboard her instead of on the London-bound train.

Sliding down that slippery rope he had entered into a life that could hardly have appealed to him more had it been made to order. A young man descended from Cornish sea dogs, growing up among fishermen, liking above all things to feel wind and salt spray in his face and the pitching deck of a boat under his feet, exulting in a lively tussle with the elements, such a man was in his proper place on a voyage like this one.

It was winter, and the North Sea promptly showed its teeth. The little ship sailed out of Yarmouth into winds that seemed to blow straight down from the Arctic Ocean. She was tossed about like a toy, and for two months her deck was glassy with ice. In the harbor of Ostend, she was ice-locked and could not stir from her moorings till a steamer had broken a path. However, this delay was quite all right with Dr. Grenfell. The ice was smooth and he had brought his skates with him.

The real excitement, also the real work for a doctor, began when they reached the fishing fleets off the Dogger Banks. Here was a great floating camp of men, living on boats instead of in tents. And they were the kind of men Wilfred Grenfell liked—plain, hearty, full of zest for life, roaring out songs of the sea as they worked, laughing at danger, laughing at each other. They reminded him of old-time buccaneers out of sea tales. He was par-

:icularly attracted by one "great, black-bearded pirate over forty-seven inches around the chest."

Nights on the North Sea were never to be forgotten. A hundred boats became a village of lights, doubled in calm weather by the water's reflections. Ship's lanterns vied with the low-hanging, winter-bright stars. Now and then rockets would go swishing up out of the darkness to fall in showers of light—signals to the fishermen from the admiral of the fleet. And how those men could sing! Their songs rang across the water through the night, while they waited for the order to haul in the net.

Sometimes the nets brought up out of the sea along with a load of live silver, relics of days long past—bones of animals that had grazed here before the sea ever broke through the English channel, a bit of crockery made in Queen Elizabeth's time, a piece of the wreckage of an ancient square-rigged vessel.

The young doctor, as he leaned over the rail of the mission boat, watching and listening, felt as if removed from the world he had known into a landless—well-nigh timeless—world hanging between sky and water. It would have hardly seemed strange if a sixteenth-century privateer commissioned by Good Queen Bess should suddenly have loomed up on the dim line between earth and sky or if word should have come that a Spanish galleon was sighted. He missed none of the beauty, none of the romance of this life. Yet he was keenly aware of its grim and sombre side.

These fishermen did not see their families or know anything of home life for two and three months at a stretch. Most of the young apprentices had no homes, having been taken into the fleet directly from reformatories. Discipline was stern, even brutally cruel at times, especially if the skipper happened to be a hard-drinking man. Cheap dives on shore and grog ships at sea robbed the men of their wages and their self-respect.

Night and day danger stood at every man's elbow. More than a dozen of the fleet's crew were sometimes swept into the sea in one day, while loading boxes of fish on a steamer for market. Perhaps the "man overboard" might bob up and be hauled on deck little the worse for a ducking in icy water. Again, he might be trapped under an over-turned boat or crushed between two boats. Then one more fisherman would be missing from the fleet.

When a man slipped on an ice-coated deck and broke a leg or an arm or when someone fell sick, there had been up to now only one thing to do for the sufferer—send him to market along with the load of fish. Men died who might just as well have lived. Men suffered needless tortures from unset bones and infected injuries, all for want of skilled care in time.

What a chance for a man like Wilfred Grenfell, with his quick sympathy, his professional skill, and his strong desire to help people, especially those who had been born to hardship and struggle. And what a friend in

...eed for the crew! They were not slow to sense his genuine liking for them, to appreciate that he was a pal as well as a doctor. Here was no London toff, no blundering land-lubber, no pompous medico, and certainly no sanctimonious meddler with their lives, but a simple man —one of themselves he seemed—who would rather be afloat with the fleet than anywhere else. They could swap yarns with this man and joke with him.

And so for several winters Grenfell sailed among the North Sea fishing fleets, bandaging wounds, splinting broken bones, prescribing medicines, being an understanding friend to men who "do business in great waters," and having, as he put it, "jolly good fun." Into those winters were packed adventures more varied than many people experience in their entire lives, adventures that were all in the day's work.

He was with the fleets off the Dogger Banks and with herring fishermen off the west coast of Ireland, where 'enough nets were set each night to reach to America and back again." He explored the Arran Islands, the Skerry Islands, and the Lewis Islands. Manxmen, Irishmen, Scotsmen, and Englishmen were his patients. One day a call for his services came from lonely Fastnet Light on a rock in the open ocean. To reach the lighthouse in a heavy sea, he had to grab a line and be swung by a crane to his patient. Again, on a trip to market with a fisherman, the boat capsized in a squall. Wet and shivering, he and his companion sought shelter within a one-room cabin set down in the middle of a bog, where a cow, a donkey, and chickens and humans all had to live together.

This was poverty more desperate than anything he had seen before, even in London slums. It was like him to offer to recompense the family for their hospitality by paying for a cattle pen. There was food for much thought in the answer that a new building would only mean a raise in rent from the landlord, with no more money coming in to pay it. How much he had been learning about poverty in the past few years.

Grenfell still grabbed opportunities to go exploring on his own and still added to the collections started so many years before. On the Arran Islands we find him clambering up precipices to pick rare ferns out of the rock crevices. Nor did he miss a chance to stop and talk with two men who sat with hooks and lines at the top of a cliff pulling fish up dizzy heights from the waters below. At the Skerry Islands, he and some other daredevils flung themselves off high cliffs into the sea, then climbed up the slippery face of them in order to reach the rock shelf where snow-white gannets nested. He just had to get some specimens of their eggs for his collection. As if this were not risking his neck enough for one day, he proceeded to drape himself down over the top of a precipice and lift one or two gull's eggs up out of a nest with a dexterous foot.

Evidently the men who employed Grenfell soon made

the same discovery that had been made quite promptly by the fishermen. This young man was not just a doctor. He was an all-round person who could handle a boat in any kind of weather, help haul a net of fish, and turn a hand to many sorts of undertakings. So the Mission began to make use of these varied abilities. One of his jobs was to set out in a trawler and sail all along the coast of Ireland to discover where the best fishing grounds were and then report back to headquarters. And they called that work! thought he, smiling to himself.

It would have been hard for Dr. Grenfell to have told which he enjoyed the more during these years—his winters or his summers. He was now medical officer for an organization known as the English Public School Camps. And so he had another working vacation in midsummer, doing for an organization somewhat the kind of thing he had organized by himself for the boys of East London. Certainly there were no happier moments in his life than some of those spent in pleasant places by the sea with a bunch of boys. And pleasant places they were—the sites of those camps.

Great country estates were opened to the campers by some of the landed gentry, who were interested in boys. Yachts were placed at their disposal as well as bathing beaches and tennis courts. Even if the memories of those summer days had not been so delightful that they lingered with him, the boys would not have allowed their doctor to forget them. For years afterward, these companions of a few weeks still bobbed up in person or by letter, just as many of those club members and campers from East London did. Sometimes an "old boy" would tell how one stay at camp had given him such a completely new start that from then on life had been all made over for him. One of these, grown extremely prosperous, appeared years later when Grenfell was on a lecture trip in America and paid an unforgotten debt of gratitude in the form of a generous contribution to the Labrador work.

The service to the North Sea fleets grew apace, till there were several mission ships instead of one and a brand-new hospital ship named for Queen Victoria, which Her Majesty had helped to buy and equip. One wonders if the enthusiastic help rendered by young Dr. Grenfell were not partly responsible for the growing reputation of the undertaking.

In 1891, the men at the head of the Royal National Mission for Deep Sea Fishermen began looking across the Atlantic to the fleets of fishing boats off Northern Newfoundland and Labrador. What about extending this work to the bleak coasts of that neglected bit of the British Empire? Thirty thousand men fished in those waters that lashed themselves to fury against bare rock shores and were iced by the Arctic Current. And there was no doctor there—no doctor and no hospital within hundreds of miles.

Thereupon Wilfred Grenfell was asked the most im-

'ortant question ever put to him, at least so far as its onsequences were concerned. Would he take a sailing hip, equip her for an overseas voyage, pick a crew, and ail across the ocean to see what could be done for these nen?

Would he?

Why, everything he had done, beginning with those ruises in *The Reptile* on the river Dee, had been fitting im for this voyage, for the life work that awaited him t the end of it. By now he was a Master Mariner as well s a doctor, and knew fishing and fishermen as thoroughly as anyone could who had not actually made a iving with nets and trawls. What he called the "frills of fe" meant nothing to him. He felt none of the urges nany men have—to accumulate a large bank account, to cquire land and a great house and things to put in a reat house. Even now while yet in his early twenties, he purpose of life seemed to him "not to have and to old but to give and to serve." No amount of money ould have tempted him to turn down a chance like this, ombining as it did adventure by land and sea and service to people whose need was great.

The mere thought of fitting out his own boat for the rip filled him with delight. What months those were— he months of anticipation and preparation! Grenfell lanned every detail of the expedition. He selected the *llbert*, a ninety-nine ton ketch-rigged schooner, and upervised all the repairs and alterations necessary to make her fit for a voyage on the open ocean. The sound of ringing hammers on the quay at Yarmouth was music in his ears. It meant that the hull was being reinforced forward with "greatheart" so that the prow could cut through ice-strewn waters. The clank-clank of metal told of the new iron hatches to replace old wooden ones. That fluttery sound heralded the unfurling of the large square sail he had ordered attached to the foremast to steady the ship in heavy weather.

With perhaps even greater care and keener pleasure, he fitted up a small hospital amidships, complete with operating table, surgical supplies, medicines, and bunks for future patients.

All these preparations took time. It was the spring of 1892 before the stout little ship was pronounced ready for high winds, rough weather, and icebergs. Next came the important business of choosing a skipper who had sailed the North Atlantic, a mate, and a crew.

The hold was filled with food, warm clothing, blankets, and all the other supplies that might be needed between May and November not only for the crew but also for those fishermen on the other side of the Atlantic.

At last a sailing date could be set.

He slid down the rope

CHAPTER EIGHT

Voyage of Discovery

A crowd was on the dock that June day when the *Albert* weighed anchor at Great Yarmouth. There were brown-faced seamen and pale landlubbers, city folk and country folk, old Parkgate friends and new friends from London. Perhaps a few ex-public-school-campers and some of those East London vacation companions were among those present. Certainly members of the old *Roysterer's* crew must have been there to wish their former skipper good-by. And of course Wilfred's mother was there.

The tanned young man who was the center of attention simply beamed with pride. What a sight—what a mighty fine sight—that small ship was with her sails unfurled. So was Captain Trevize, the stern and leathery-looking Cornishman he had chosen for skipper. As for Joe White, the mate, and the rest of the crew, they were old friends, tried companions of many a North Sea voyage. It was good fun to show off his trim craft and to introduce the ship's company to the friends who had come to see him off for Labrador. Look at those timbers and her iron hatches! She'll take storms and icebergs like a Viking's boat. Solid teakwood decks, too. And now come below and see my floating hospital. How would you like to be in charge of a tidy little dispensary like this, doctor? Well, mother, what do you think of the *Albert*? Yes, it was a proud day for Dr. Grenfell.

Did the extremely business-like captain, to whom this was just another voyage instead of a great adventure, grow impatient with all the talk and fuss? 'Tis likely. At least he must have been considerably relieved when the tugboat began nudging and shoving at the *Albert's* stout sides, and when the good ship's prow at last pointed south toward the Straits of Dover.

"Good luck, Doctor!" "A fine trip to you, Grenfell!" "Good-by, Wilfred!" The shouts grew louder as an expanse of water appeared between pier and boat. Then they became fainter and fainter, and presently waving hands carried the good wishes that could not be heard. The doctor stood on deck and swung his cap like a banner, while the breezes caught the Union Jack and the blue Mission flag and spread them against the sky.

A voyage of discovery had begun.

No voyager of old sent forth into uncharted seas with a patent from his king or queen could have felt more like one on great explorations bound than did Wilfred Grenfell on that morning in June. He reminded himself how he was following the same course John Cabot had steered four centuries before and that his ship was just about the size of the *Matthew* in which Cabot had sailed out of Bristol Harbor.

The hopes and dreams of that old-time explorer were wholly different from those of this nineteenth century physician. Great possessions for his king and for himself had Cabot sought, and the fame and royal favor that such discoveries would bring him. He had read Marco Polo's glittering descriptions of the Land of the Great Khan and the riches therein. Like Columbus, he looked for a new route to the treasures of Asia.

As for Grenfell, about the only trait he had in common with John Cabot was a great liking for adventure. He was well aware that a poverty-stricken coast lay at the end of his voyage, but he also knew that a job entirely to his liking waited for him. In a sense he *was* a real explorer. Before the voyage of the *Albert*, almost no one knew much about Labrador. It was just a strip of land on the map.

Suppose, among that company of friends gathered at Yarmouth in 1892, there had been a seer who could have looked into the years ahead. Suppose he had prophesied, "Grenfell, for your work in Labrador you will be known not only in England but all over the United States and Canada and in many other parts of the world. Greater honors will be yours than ever were bestowed upon a

71

voyager of old, and in the fullness of time you will be knighted by a king."

Well, the young doctor would certainly have laughed heartily in the face of such a prophet. Fame was the last thing he expected to win by doctoring poor fishermen off the Labrador coast.

On that June day and during all the nineteen days of the voyage, there was little time for speculations about the future. Apparently Nature at once made it quite clear that a trip to Labrador was no vacation cruise. Right off the south coast of Ireland, the small ship battled mountainous seas, and all the way across the Atlantic it pushed against head winds. For three days dense fog dropped impenetrable curtains around the *Albert*, wrapping everyone and everything in its clammy folds. Suddenly an icy chill rose from the water, a chill that meant just one thing—icebergs. Fog and icebergs—the combination most dreaded by mariners! Now one of those glittering ice castles loomed up straight in front of the prow. The man who was steering stopped breathing and swung the wheel literally for his life. The *Albert* swerved, missing a crash by what looked like inches. Now for several days the way led through a squadron of icebergs. Hours at the wheel meant tense watching for danger every instant. The midsummer breezes were cold as winds of winter.

When the fog lifted, it revealed, like a raised stage curtain, a new scene—majestic cliffs topped by dark green woods, a lighthouse, rocky headlands. This was the shore of Newfoundland, the "new found land" discovered by Cabot. Shouts of delight rose from the little company. There is no experience that compares for excitement with catching the first glimpse of a foreign shore. A new world is opening before one's eyes, a world of unlimited possibilities for adventure. After an ocean voyage of nearly three weeks on a little sailing ship, that sight of a new land offers thrills no traveler on a swift comfortable liner can ever know. And this was a coast of rare beauty—beautiful and awe-inspiring in its lone majesty. It dared the stranger. It warned him to approach at his own risk.

"Where are we?" the crew asked excitedly.

"Just north of St. John's," was the answer. There was a gleam of satisfaction in Grenfell's eyes. In spite of head winds, heavy seas, fog, and icebergs, the *Albert* had come almost to the exact spot planned for the first landing place, the capital city of Newfoundland.

The questioners stared doubtfully at those iron-black 500-foot cliffs. As far south as they could see stretched a seemingly unbroken wall of rocks. Where was the city? How was it possible for a ship to land anywhere on such a defiant shore?

There was, they were told, a narrow opening in the wall, so narrow that during the French and Indian Wars the French closed it to the English with chains, like a gate.

The *Albert* turned toward the southeast, looking as if she were heading for a certain crash against a precipice. She rounded a headland, and there between two great rock gateposts was the six-hundred-foot opening to a harbor that reached inland for a mile. What a sight now met the eyes of the men on the ship staring ahead for a first glimpse of St. John's!

Clouds of smoke rose from the rocky hills, enveloping the buildings that still clung to them. Naked chimneys loomed up in rows like black monuments, marking where houses, churches, and warehouses had stood a few hours ago. Here and there among the forest of masts along shore one mast blazed like an enormous torch. The air that blew offshore was like a blast from an open furnace. St. John's was being swept by the worst fire in its whole history. This voyage seemed destined to encounter obstacles and delays.

However, inopportune though the time of arrival was, the little company received a warm welcome. A doctor had come from England specially to look after the men "down North on the Labrador!" Everyone in the city knew how much that would mean.

Grenfell's work of relieving suffering began at once. The warm clothing and blankets stowed away on the *Albert* would never be needed more. They were unpacked and distributed among those who had lost everything and medicines were given away to the sick. Of course the voyage to Labrador was delayed. No busi-

74

ness could be transacted and no pilot for that dangerous coastwise trip could be secured until the fires had stopped raging and the homeless were looked after.

Meanwhile the doctor's eyes and ears were hard at work. He visited every ship in the harbor and chatted with their crews, absorbing all the information about fishing and fishermen that could be extracted from the men of St. John's. He had a chance to talk with old salts who had fished off Labrador in years past, with the wives of men who were down there this season, and with old "swilers"—those who went seal-hunting every spring when the big satiny creatures appeared off the northern coast.

What tales some of those men and women had to tell —tales of ships battered against rocks, torn open, and sunk before help could reach them, of death and narrow escapes from death by drowning, by freezing, and by starvation. Never a year that some craft was not dashed to pieces. Had the doctor ever noticed how a fisherman's hands were bent? Yes, his keen eyes had not missed the fact that the hands of these men of the coast were never quite flattened out like a landsman's. Well, that was because a man who did business in these waters was forever having to grab hold of a rock or a spar or something else and cling to it like a crab.

They talked of people starving. Wasn't there food enough for everybody down north?

Not in the winter-time on the Labrador. The liveyeres

75

had hard picking then. Sometimes for months flour and water was all they had even for the babies.

The "liveyeres?" Who were they?

Why, they were the folks that lived there all the year round. There were some four thousand of them. Indians lived in Labrador too, and farther north Eskimos. "Starvation coast," folks called that northern shore, and a good name for it.

There was an old saying that the Lord made the world in five days, made Labrador on the sixth, and spent Sunday throwing stones at it.

Didn't those "liveyeres" raise anything to eat, not even potatoes? Didn't they keep cows or pigs?

There wasn't much place to plant stuff, except on rocks. What little dirt could be scratched together didn't thaw out till July. As for raising a cow or a pig, well they guessed the doctor didn't know much about huskies. "Them dogs was just like wolves, when it came to killing and eating other critters."

Where did the men in the fishing fleet come from?

From 'most everywhere—all up and down the coast and from Nova Scotia. Some of them even sailed out of Gloucester and Boston—all that way. Some brought their families and some "batched it."

Yes, there was plenty to learn about Labrador. The doctor began to glimpse problems that he had not been expecting. When he was not asking questions or listening, we can imagine him doing a great deal of looking about. Now he squinted through his binoculars at a wide-winged bird with a white head and tail that floated above the cliffs. It may have been the first bald eagle he had ever seen. Again he noted the grace of an arctic tern, as it dropped from sky to sea, or he smiled at the humorous aspect of "sea parrots with their huge red noses, standing cheek by jowl on the edge of a precipice."

Very likely he got out his sketchbook and made hasty little drawings of the cliffs and the birds to keep or tuck into a letter to a friend. It was a habit of his.

Yet in spite of all there was to learn here, Grenfell must have grown impatient to be off. All that was told him added to his eagerness to see this unfriendly land of fog and rocks that was his goal. How warmly he welcomed Captain Nicholas Fitzgerald, the pilot, when finally he climbed aboard and the *Albert* sailed out of the harbor and headed Northwest! Again the course lay among menacing icebergs, and now there were rocky islands of all shapes and sizes and, worse still, hidden reefs to avoid.

For four days and four nights nothing was to be seen but gray fog. Life aboard ship went on to the continual dolorous sound of the foghorn. The only safety was in keeping well out to sea. The doctor began to understand why shipwrecks and sudden death were taken for granted by the men who fished and trafficked off this hostile coast. The old fishermen of St. John's had told

77

no tall tales about life "down north." If ever a land warned men to keep off, Labrador did.

Yet the strongest impression made upon Grenfell's senses by the first glimpse he caught of Labrador was one of utter beauty. Never before had he witnessed such wild beauty on land or sea, as greeted his eyes when the *Albert* put in toward the shore. That picture he saw early on the morning of August fourth, 1892, was so perfectly photographed on his mind that it never faded. Forty years later he would recall the tints of sea and rocks and sky exactly as they were that day—how green the top of Round Hill Island was, how pink were its cliffs, the white line where the breakers marked off the green sea from the rosy rocks, the silver streak made by a leaping fish. And he would hear again the whales slapping the water sportively with their tails, the thunder of the Atlantic against those ancient unyielding rocks, and the sea birds crying from the ledges.

There and then Wilfred Grenfell fell completely under the spell of this untamed shore. Henceforth its perils and discomforts would seem trifling compared with its delights. Henceforth he would never be content to remain long away from Labrador and in no other place would he ever feel so thoroughly alive.

The thought that Round Hill Island probably at no time had been inhabited by man delighted him. There was also a thrill in surmising that this was the first land sighted by Cabot. The hills that rose one behind another

78

along the mainland, the small islands like perilous stepping stones to the coast, the inlets that invited the voyager to come and see what lay within them, all these things appealed to the explorer in Grenfell. On that August morning, the ghosts of those Cornish ancestors probably decided once and for all that this young man was worthy to bear their name.

The ship turned and made for an opening between a pink cliff and a green island, carefully negotiating a mountainous iceberg that almost closed the entrance to Domino Run. Grenfell found himself in a long narrow creek. Perched on the rocks along the shore were fish stages, where cod lay drying, and turf huts and wooden shacks roofed with turf. How many boats there were— nearly a hundred, he would say. On the schooners were bronzed men in blue jerseys cutting up bait and mending nets. The long voyage to Labrador was ended.

Now it was the Labrador men who were excited. They stared open-mouthed. Where did this boat come from? Not from anywhere along the coast. They could tell that from the cut of her sails. What was she doing in this little run? She carried no net and no dory; so she wasn't after fish. She couldn't be a trader. There was no sign of barrels of oil or boxes of salt. She flew the Union Jack, but what was that blue flag with words on it in white? They couldn't read, and anyway the name "Royal National Mission for Deep Sea Fishermen" would have meant nothing to them. Now she was dropping anchor.

Well, they'd give her a welcome whatever she wanted. From one little boat after another a flag of greeting was run up to flutter in the early morning light.

A doctor who goes to a strange place to practice usually has to "hang out his shingle" and then sit back and twiddle his thumbs for weeks while possible patients are discovering him and making up their minds about him. It took these fishermen less than five minutes to discover Dr. Grenfell.

"It's a doctor. He's come yere on purpose to take care o' we." The message flew from boat to boat and from one fisherman to another, almost as swiftly as if a breeze carried the words or a telegraph ticked them out. Dipping oars splashed. The dories began to cluster around the *Albert,* bringing word of this one on such and such a boat who had been ailing all summer and that one on shore who "needed a doctor bad." Men kept asking, "Can ye haul teeth?"

A starved-looking, ragged young man came alongside in a rowboat that looked as if it would drop to pieces. He sat staring and said nothing. "Be you a real doctor?" he asked finally, as if such a thing couldn't be true. "Us has no money, but there's a very sick man ashore. Be you a real doctor?"

They rowed across to a turf hut. Grenfell was not particularly tall, but he had to stoop to enter the low door of that hovel. For a moment he could see almost nothing in the dim light of the one small opening covered with a crazy patchwork of broken pieces of glass stuck together. When his eyes grew accustomed to the dimness, it was all he could do to keep from crying out at the sight that met them. Could human beings live like this? The place was no better than a ground-hog's hole. There was one damp chilly room with pebbles for a floor. A rusty stove and wooden bunks built along the sides were its only furniture.

In one of the bunks lay a man burning up with fever and literally coughing his life away. A woman dressed in rags was doing all she could for him—that is, she poured sips of cold water down his throat from time to time. Six neglected children shrank into a corner at the entrance of a stranger.

If only he had come this way sooner! Or if there were a hospital and a nurse somewhere near! Never before had Dr. Grenfell felt quite so powerless to help another. What a hollow pretense it was to leave medicine here. He could add some food for the mother and children. Yet that too seemed almost futile. "The fish were in," and the one man in the family was not out catching them. The best of the year's earnings were being lost. Sickness in a land where only the able-bodied could earn was not misfortune; it was grim tragedy.

If only the *Albert* had sailed sooner, he kept thinking! The accumulated ills of months—even of years—awaited the coming of Wilfred Grenfell.

CHAPTER NINE

"I'll Be Back"

"Good-by. I'll be back."

"Keep your wrist bandaged for another week, Jimmy."

"Good luck, Uncle Joe. You'll be capering about on that leg by the time I'm here again in the spring."

It was late October. The *Albert*, her prow now pointed southward toward St. John's, was still sailing in and out of coves and "runs" and "tickles." It was hard for Grenfell to say good-by to Labrador. In two months he had doctored nine hundred people. Yet that amazing record did not satisfy him. So much was left to be done. Other men, women, and children needed care just as much as any of those nine hundred. Yet he could not possibly reach them before the coast was locked against boats by ice. And he must visit again some of those sickest patients. How could he sail home without knowing whether or not they were still alive?

"We'll wake up some fine morning and find ourselves frozen in here!" warned Captain Trevize.

"In just a few days now I'll be through. But I must top at the next cove and see the McDonald baby again. Iis mother doesn't know how to take care of that ear f his. And I'll have to put in at Domino Run." How vere the family in that dark little hut? The father must ave died. Did the mother and her children have anyhing to eat? Yes, it was terribly hard to leave.

A few nights later the Northern Lights were in carival mood. They threw red and green and golden treamers across the sky till Dr. Grenfell and his crew asped at the wild beauty above and around them. Fhe boat's prow left a trail of cold fire in the phosphoresent waters and the leaping fish glowed as if dipped in ght.

" 'Twill be colder tomorrow," prophesied the anxious Japtain.

In the morning the doctor came up from his beforereakfast dip a little blue. "Br-r-r." There were gleamig jewels all along the *Albert's* water line and a border f fringed ice outlined the shore and framed every rock. n another day the fishermen had to cut through ice two iches deep to reach open sea. There could be little more ngering to visit this one and that one. 'Twas time to o home.

What would they say in St. John's, when he told them bout his summer's work and all he wanted to do next ummer—with their help? Hospitals, he must have buildigs for hospitals, and he must bring with him doctors and nurses next time. This was no one-man job. If only those fisherfolk could cry out from their boats and miserable huts so that all the world might hear them! But they were used to suffering in silence and they were far away. Anyway, the world should hear *about* them. He was going to see to that, and he would begin in St. John's. The men there who profited by the fisheries, surely they would be willing to help build a hospital for the men who caught the fish for them.

Within the rock walls of St. John's harbor, one of the happiest surprises of Wilfred Grenfell's life awaited him. His fame had gone before him on the wings of fishing schooners. Home-going men had told, with wonder in their eyes, about this "Dr. Grandfield" or "Granfel"— whatever his name was. He had made the lame walk. He had cured folks who had been ailing for years. The whole thing was as much of a miracle as if 'twere "right out of the Good Book itself," they said.

The city received him as an honored guest. "There was a piece in the paper about you," men on the docks told him. "We know what's been going on down there," said the business men. The Board of Trade was impressed. So was the Governor of Newfoundland, Sir Terence O'Brien. His Excellency proceeded to call a meeting of leading citizens at Government House in the doctor's honor. They passed a resolution expressing the thanks of the Colony "for the amount of medical and surgical work done" by this doctor from overseas. They

Burning of Saint John's

formally requested that he come again to these shores and keep up the work so ably begun, and pledged the cooperation of the colony.

What a day that was for Dr. Grenfell! It had never occurred to him that anyone here would have heard about his summer's work till he arrived and told people what he had done. The men of St. John's were not just talking, either. By the time the *Albert* put out to sea, a committee had been appointed by the Governor to help the Royal Mission and a house at Battle Harbor, just beyond the Straits of Belle Isle, had been donated by a local fishery firm as Labrador's first hospital. The doctor's resolve was already coming true. The world had begun to hear about Labrador.

They were a happy ship's company—the men who embarked for home in November on that small boat. Happiest of all of them was Wilfred Grenfell. Not even as a boy had he been in higher spirits, not when the pony had appeared at Mostyn House, not on the shores of the Mediterranean. 'Twas bitter cold. The winds were angry. Great cliffs of water piled up behind the *Albert*. To prevent the boat from being swamped, the crew filled canvas bags with cod-liver oil, made drip holes in them, and hung the bags from the spinnaker boom. The oil spread over the water and smoothed it out a little. Yet laughter rang out, as the men climbed icy ropes that swung in the wind like cobwebs and walked a heaving, slippery deck.

When the weather was not too boisterous, hilarious games of cricket were played on deck. And when the last ball went overboard, over the rail went the doctor after it. Ah! but that was a gay voyage—the home-going voyage of the *Albert*.

Yet, in quiet hours alone, Grenfell grew extremely serious, working on his report to the council of the Mission and making long, long plans for Labrador. Sometimes he seemed to hear again above the slapping of waves and the flapping of canvas the voices of men and women talking in that queer Labrador dialect.

"We doant want she to die." That woman was alive and taking care of her family now.

"I split a dried herring and tied it round his t'roat, but the little lad choked hisself to death." He could see the poor father's face. The fisherman had done the best he knew how, but the "little lad" with diphtheria needed more than a herring poultice to cure him. What wouldn't the doctor give if he might have come in time to save that choking child!

"I tried deer's marrow, sir. I washed it with tansy water and rubbed it with shark's gall, but it's still bad and I doant know what to do." What a tough baby to have survived having all that dirty stuff rubbed on an open sore!

"What can you'se do for us?" asked the blind pathetically. They were so utterly useless in a land of fishing

and trapping. He must somehow get an eye specialist over there to lift the "curtains" from those eyes.

Louder than all the other voices, he heard the young man in the boat asking, *"Be you a real doctor?"*

The picture of that man and many other pictures kept rising before him. A little girl cuddled a bundle of rags, calling it her "dolly," while a cheap doll bought from a trader sat on a shelf high above the reach of short arms. "I had to put it away," the mother explained. "Her kissed it so much her most wore the paint off." What a joy it would be to load a ship with a cargo of nothing but dolls and cruise up and down the coast—a seagoing Santa Claus! Well, he would certainly bring back a trunkful.

He recalled a baby he had seen, dressed in nothing but an old trouser leg, toddling about, as awkward as a man running a sack race. He should have a little suit, when the *Albert* came back next summer.

There were pleasant pictures as well as pathetic ones. Those bronzed men in blue jerseys and sea boots hauling their nets, tireless as vikings, what a sight they were! He could hear them singing lustily to the strains of an accordion—

> "Jack was ev'ry inch a sailor,
> Five and twenty years a wha-a-ler;
> Jack was ev'ry inch a sailor,
> He was born upon the bright blue sea."

Sometimes it seemed to the doctor as if he had been born "upon the bright blue sea," instead of at Mostyn House.

There had been a merry scene on the *Albert* one day. A couple in a remote spot had come to the doctor and asked if he would "say a few words over them." There happened to be a minister on shipboard at the time; so an impromptu wedding was arranged. The whole ship's company entered into the spirit of the occasion, even serving a wedding breakfast of hardtack and tea.

Seascapes and landscapes flashed in succession before his eyes. Again the land and sea viewed from a high hill melted together and looked like a "giant opal." Icebergs, picked out of the blackness by lightning in a terrific thunder storm, glittered in awesome splendor before his eyes. The unearthly lights of the aurora borealis filled him with wonder, even as remembered beauty—the "merry dancers," the Labrador people called them.

Surely he was an explorer, and this had been as much of a voyage of discovery as ever the Cabots made. Nobody had really *seen* this coast before—all its misery, all its beauty, all its possibilities.

The Voyage of the Princess May

"How big was that baby, Wilfred?"

"About so big—but he'll have grown a lot by next summer."

Mrs. Grenfell had just been hearing about the baby who wore a trouser leg, and she was now making a beeline for her sewing basket and scrap bag. That new suit was already as good as made.

It was December. Wilfred Grenfell was back at Mostyn House, talking a blue streak about all that had befallen him since that day in June when he had put out from Great Yarmouth. Was it, could it be, only six months ago?

"We'll go boat hunting up the river," suggested Algernon with enthusiasm. His brother had been telling how much he wanted to find a steam launch that would nose into little coves where the *Albert* couldn't go and tow the sailboat when there was no breeze blowing.

The years seemed to roll back when the two of them

went prowling along the banks of the Dee. Once more the young doctor hobnobbed with the fishermen of Parkgate. Now his tales topped any sea stories or fish stories they could tell. Again he heard people call him "Wilfred" instead of "Dr. Grenfell." Again he hunted for birds in the marshes. It was like old times. Yet everything was different, too. The Dee seemed to have shrunk somewhat in size. So had the blue hills in Wales; they did not look so high or so mysterious as they used to. The long stretch of salt marshes was less vast than in childhood days. There had been a time when those waving reeds grew, it seemed, to the edge of the world. How snug and trimmed and oh! how green England was after Labrador. Good though it was to be home, only half of Wilfred Grenfell was here on the Dee. The other half was cruising along a rocky, ice-strewn coast.

This young man who had come home for the winter was even busier than the ever-busy boy Wilfred had been. He started right in to let the world hear about Labrador. Next to be told his story after Mrs. Grenfell and Algernon, was Sir Frederick Treves. The great surgeon was as proud of his former pupil as if he had been his own son. Nine hundred patients treated! An urgent request from His Excellency the Governor of Newfoundland that the Mission send their Dr. Grenfell back! A hospital promised! All this had been accomplished in a few months. When, in February, word came from St. John's that a second fishery company had offered to build a hospital for the Mission at Indian Harbor, the fruits of one summer's work of one man seemed truly amazing.

The thing that pleased Sir Frederick most was that this unusual young doctor had found a life work big enough for him: so broad, so deep, so high that he could put into it all his talents, his greatheartedness and sympathy. The older man had only to look into Wilfred Grenfell's eyes as he talked of Labrador to know that this was true.

There were many others that must hear about plans and hopes for Labrador—childhood friends, friends who had helped to make possible those camping trips, friends who had backed the Public School camps. He just had to tell them how men, women, and children of their own breed, fellow-subjects of their Queen, were dying in far-off coves and harbors from Cape Bauld to Cape Chidley. Having touched their hearts, he tackled their pocketbooks. He must take back with him next summer two doctors and two nurses for those new hospitals. He had to get hold of an X-ray machine somehow, and that little steam launch, and any amount of clothing and quantities of tinned milk for the puny babies, the rickety children, and the tubercular.

People listened in amazement to the stories the young doctor told that winter, the sights he described. Could these things be in this year of grace eighteen hundred ninety-three? Why, the worst slums of London could not reveal such poverty and suffering! They were greatly moved by the simple sincerity of the young man. Before the winter was over, he was sure of money enough to pay two doctors and two nurses, to buy an X-ray machine and an old boat.

The boat hunt with Algernon really was like childhood days. This time he had to have a craft more seaworthy than the *Reptile* or the *Roysterer*. They found near home a little old steam launch, lying idle on the race course at Chester and looking rather forlorn, as unused boats do. "How about this one?" asked Algernon. "She's just the right size, but she'll take some fixing," Wilfred decided.

"I can do the fixing," volunteered the older brother, who liked to fuss around with hammer and nails and paint and brush as well as he had in the days when he helped build the *Reptile* and hammered cases together for the boys' collections.

Having learned that the old boat could be bought for a fair price, the next step was to find someone who would put up the price. "She'll go anywhere. She'll double the number of patients I can get to," he told one of his old friends. "And I won't have to stop for head winds or for calms or anything else." There followed an eloquent description of delays and difficulties that had beset the *Albert*, ending with a determined, "I've simply got to cover more ground next summer." By the time Grenfell had finished, the friend could fairly see

"Be you a real doctor?"

Towering cliffs rose in front of them

people waiting for that boat to come. "I'll buy it for you," he agreed.

Algernon had a wonderful time caulking her seams, patching, and painting her. "She's a beauty," declared his brother when they launched her on the Dee. Then the brothers went chug-chugging merrily on a little trip across the river to the Canal into the Mersey River and down the Mersey to Liverpool. There they had to watch her being slung unceremoniously onto the deck of a liner bound for St. John's.

How small she looked up there—like a toy! "Never mind," Wilfred felt like saying to the snubbed launch, "wait till I get you to Labrador and see how important you are there. You'll be busier and loaded down with more of a cargo than any boat that ever sailed the Dee or the Mersey. I'll show you icebergs and whales too, little lady, and rocks that are rocks."

On May 6, 1893, there was a great blowing of whistles and running up of flags in St. John's harbor. "I christen thee the *Princess May;* God speed thee on thy way," rang out the voice of Her Excellency, Lady O'Brien. The little boat from Chester that was only eight feet wide had become a princess, named for the princess who was destined to be England's Queen Mary. A cablegram from the lady herself had granted gracious consent to the naming of this new Mission boat for her. It was really enough to turn the head of a river launch.

In the midst of the festivities, many of the old salts

shook their heads doubtfully. They kept on with their head-shaking, while the doctor stoked her engine with wood as if it were a big kitchen stove, and started North in her.

"He'll never make it in that boat," they agreed, "not t'rough all the ice." The English doctor was a fine chap, but it seemed like he didn't know how to be afraid of anything.

The subject of these remarks, undismayed, chugged out of the harbor into the ice-strewn sea. Having crossed the ocean in the *Albert*, he was now off for Labrador in his own launch. He had a cook and an engineer, plenty of food, and a great pile of wood to feed the *Princess*. He'd bring her through. How did that song go he had heard men singing at St. John's?

> "O, Lukey's boat is painted green
> Aha, me b'ys,
> O, Lukey's boat is painted green,
> The prettiest little boat ever you seen.
> Aha, me riddle I day."

Ahead of the *Princess May*, on the *Albert*, were two doctors and two nurses. Yes, they were actually here. It still didn't seem possible that he had a staff. What couldn't he do this summer! The new hospital at Battle Harbor was all ready for them, and a second one was being built. "Aha, me riddle I day."

The Voyage of the Princess May

As he sawed wood for the boiler of the ever-hungry *Princess* or steered her in and out among bergs and submerged rocks, the doctor made plans for a summer of tremendous accomplishment. While the *Albert* visited the larger villages, he would seek the out-of-the-way places that had been neglected last summer. He would explore the coast thoroughly from Cape Bauld to Cape Mugford, where only Eskimos lived.

"Bang! Scra-ape! Scra-ape!" They were on a rock. After much pushing and shoving, they got the *Princess* off. Then she began to settle. "She's sprung a leak," the engineer reported. "Shall we put back?"

"Put back? No. We'll plug it up."

So they plugged the hole and went on. The doctor made note of the exact location of that hidden rock for the map of this coast that he had started. They must bear further out to sea, he decided, turning the wheel, as he thought, toward the open ocean. Out of the fog a towering cliff rose in front of them. The launch missed it by barely a yard. Yet, according to the compass, they were going away from the shore, not toward it. Something was wrong with that compass. The doctor unscrewed it, and the needle swung clear around. Those iron screws had deflected the needle. Whew! That was a close call.

On they went, battling against a heavy swell. Again the *Princess May* landed on a reef, but they got her clear without damage. In these struggles, she consumed so

95

much fuel that wood-cutting was practically a continuous performance. Yet she pulled through. A week after the departure from St. John's amidst gloomy prophecies, she steamed into Battle Harbor with all hands aboard.

There stood the new hospital ready for business. It had sixteen beds waiting for the patients that would be gathered up by the *Albert* and the *Princess May*. No one, who had not worked singlehanded on the coast of Labrador with only a ship's cabin for a hospital, could possibly know what that modest frame house meant to Dr. Grenfell. If he had had a place like this last summer, perhaps that wretched man in Domino Run might have been saved! Oh well, there was no use in thinking about last summer. This was a brand new summer, and he had two nurses, two doctors, one hospital ready and another being built, and two boats.

"The doctor's come back! The doctor's come back!" the fishermen called from boat to boat. " 'Tis the doctor, the English doctor," the women told each other, as they salted and spread out cod on the fish stages.

In one cove a little redheaded boy hobbled about, with one of his feet twisted upside down. "How would you like to have me make that foot as good as the other?" asked Dr. Grenfell.

The little fellow looked at him with wondering eyes. "Could you do *that* with a pill?" he asked.

"No. Not with a pill."

"Could you charm it away, sir?"

"Yes, if you'll come to the hospital with me and let me put you to sleep."

The boy came along, even after he knew that the "charming" process would be slow and a little painful. So the doctor began picking them up and steaming to Battle Harbor with them—the crippled, the sick, the blind.

Like the fishermen of St. John's, many up and down the coast shook their heads when they saw him defying fog and gales, putting out when they, themselves, stayed close to shore. Maybe the Lord looked after him specially, they decided, because "he's so good to we."

Farther and farther north the *Princess May* nosed her way in the ice-strewn waters. Now the mountains rose straight from the shore to majestic heights. The bays were sharp gashes cut deep into cliffs, as magnificent as the fiords of Norway. Spruces, firs, and larch trees clothed the shore with fragrant beauty. The Northern Lights were visions of heaven. Ah! this was country after Wilfred Grenfell's own heart. "Never in my life had I expected any journey half so wonderful," he wrote later of this trip.

Presently he came to a village where dwelt a small, quaint-looking people with bright dark eyes. He was in the land of Eskimos. Even more than the fishermen farther south, they needed his help. In their dim huts, tuberculosis raged like the plagues of the Middle Ages. Babies died like insects. To die of old age was a rare privilege.

Yet, miserably as they lived, these were the happiest people he had ever met.

How Dr. Grenfell enjoyed their laughter and gaiety, the songs they sang, the tunes their brass bands played. The Eskimos in turn liked this doctor who had come from over the sea, they knew not where. The twinkle in his eye, the little jokes he played, the way he joined in their songs, endeared him to these fun-loving folks as much as did his kindliness. When he threw on a sheet lantern slides of themselves and played victrola records he had made of their singing, the delight and wonder in their brown faces was beautiful to see.

This northern coast was a great place for a collector, and Dr. Grenfell was as much of a collector as ever young Wilfred had been. He found flowers here that grew nowhere else and birds that never strayed farther below the Arctic Sea than these icy waters. He learned to paddle an Eskimo kayak and in it explored small inlets and shallow streams that invited him to enter them.

If it had been hard to leave Labrador before, it was three times as hard when that second fall came. The *Princess May* was the last of all the boats to start south for the winter. When autumn winds began to howl threats of gales to come, good friends in St. John's began watching for the return of the doctor. "We'll never set eyes on him again," prophesied a gloomy one. " 'Tis what I've been saying all summer," agreed another pessimist. "And he's so young, too. "Yes, young and rash."

The Voyage of the Princess May

One day in November a schooner sailed into St. John's harbor bringing a broken flagstaff from which floated a blue banner—the doctor's flag. The sight of that wet, bedraggled piece of blue cloth brought consternation to the city. The *Princess May,* christened so joyously six months ago, must have gone to pieces on a reef or berg. There had been storms and great winds lately. Had the doctor gone to the bottom? Or was he starving and freezing on some reef?

The captain of the mail boat was told to explore every cove on his trip north and to ask everyone he saw for news of the little launch and her skipper. The doctor must be found if he were alive. Captain Taylor's heart was heavy as he put out. Neither he nor anyone in the city had much expectation of seeing the young Englishman again.

"Great anxiety is felt here in regard to the fate of Dr. Grenfell," reported all the London papers on the morning of November first, quoting a cablegram received from St. John's. ". . . Dr. Grenfell left Battle Harbor, Labrador, on October 18th, in the steam launch *Princess May* bound direct for St. John's. The *Princess May* hasn't been heard of since, and grave fears are entertained for her safety as bad weather has prevailed lately off Labrador." The cable went on with the information that the mail steamer was searching for the missing doctor.

What news that was for Wilfred Grenfell's mother to

read with her morning cup of tea! What agony it must have been to sit and wait day after day for another cable. And how did Algernon feel? He had been almost a partner in this voyage of the launch from the river Dee.

"Ahoy! The *Princess May!*" You could have heard the shout that went up from the mail steamer for miles. Rounding Cape St. John, the Captain spied the little launch in Tilt Cove, where her skipper was cheerfully coaling up for the rest of the voyage.

"Thank God! Thank God!" cried Captain Taylor. "We all thought you were gone." On finding Dr. Grenfell alive and neither half-starved nor half-frozen, he gave him a great hug as if he had found a long lost son.

As for the doctor, he had fought storms and head winds. In the heavy seas, the *Princess* had rolled like a log. Her compass as well as her flag had been washed overboard. On went Dr. Grenfell, with nothing to steer by. Then he ran out of fuel and had to burn the cabin top to his boat in order to reach St. Anthony, the northernmost village of Newfoundland. There he lay up for a fortnight to make repairs. Somehow it had never occurred to him that his absence would cause such consternation. He was sorry to have given the Captain and all the others anxiety and trouble.

On November tenth, the London papers again carried a cable from Newfoundland:

"Dr. Grenfell, the chief physician of the Deep Sea

The Voyage of the Princess May

Mission to the fishing colonies in Labrador, concerning whose safety considerable anxiety was felt, has arrived here after a wonderful voyage of over six hundred miles, mostly stormy weather, in the little steam yacht, *Princess May.*"

The doctor agreed with that cablegram—it had been a "wonderful voyage."

What did the *Princess May* think about it all? Perhaps after a quiet life on the river Dee, she too, like her happy skipper, welcomed a summer as chock-full of excitement as this one had been.

CHAPTER ELEVEN

Paid in Full

Dr. Grenfell talked about his "big fees." What did he mean? Not at all what most doctors mean by fees. He was paid a modest salary, and that was all he received or expected to receive for his work.

The people of Labrador paid for medicines and hospital expenses, when they could and as they could. One woman, who had no money, insisted that the doctor take one of her sheep—she had but five, and those were all the livestock she owned. " 'Tis little enough to pay for they're saving my life down to the hospital," she said. A pat of butter, a rooster, a sack of potatoes, a mess of fish, wild-goose feathers for hospital pillows, and a day's work—in such currency was the Mission often paid.

Yet these contributions were not what Dr. Grenfell referred to as his fees. What, then, *did* he mean? Sometimes it was the look in a man's face.

"Will my little lad ever walk again, Doctor? Will 'e?"

"Walk! Why, he'll run and skip like any other boy."

At these words, tears trickled down the deep seams in the father's weathered cheeks. He wiped them away hastily with the sleeve of his blue jersey. Could it be possible that his boy would be well? He had lain a helpless cripple and in pain for months, ever since a great gale had hurled him against the rocks alongshore. Then this doctor had come in a boat and carried him to the hospital. Already he could stand up for a few minutes at a time, and the thin face that had been old with pain was round and child-like again. How the little fellow whooped with delight to find that he wouldn't have to stay in bed any more. In a land where men live by fishing and trapping, a cripple has no place, no chance to be anything but a useless burden.

Had this father pulled a handful of gold out of his pocket, Dr. Grenfell would not have felt any more richly rewarded than he did by those tears and by the look in the face of the small patient.

Would he ever forget the old man who rushed aboard the hospital boat, flung his arms around his neck, crying, "I'm the man you'se carried to the hospital teetotally blind."

There were two other blind men he was to remember as long as he lived. Each was brought to St. Anthony from a different village. Each had lost the sight of both eyes from cataracts. After the doctor had operated on them, the two fishermen, their eyes bandaged, convalesced together on the pleasant hospital sun porch, comparing notes on their operations. The day of days came. The bandages were lifted from their eyes. They looked into each other's faces. "Jim, is't you?" "George!" roared out the other. They were brothers, who had lost track of one another for years. Tucked away in different coves, separated by miles of rocky shore, unable either to read or write letters, neither had known whether the other old man was alive or dead. It was a day of miracles. To have their sight restored and then to see each other again!

Grenfell found a young girl lying helpless in her home. For fourteen years her legs had been paralyzed, and she had been like a little old lady, taking no part in the life around her. For fourteen years her busy mother had tended her. Then this doctor from England had come sailing into the cove. She hadn't half believed that he could perform an operation that would put feeling and strength back into her legs. Still folks *did* tell of marvelous things he had done. Well, she would go to that hospital of his. So they carried the crippled girl— thin and white and inert—onto the doctor's boat, and he sailed away with her.

It seemed that surely a miracle as wonderful as those of old had been performed, when after a long stay in the hospital those once-useless legs actually supported her weight. Dr. Grenfell saw that first look of joy and wonder in her eyes. Later he visited her, back home in the cottage on the rocks. She was helping her mother in the kitchen. She was scrambling in and out of boats, picking wild cranberries, having fun with her brothers and sisters. He made a mental note that he had been paid in full.

The inexpressible relief in the face of a dying man, when assured that his wife and children would be taken care of after he "had gone home"—such pay lasted long after fees in money would have been spent.

Often there would rise before the doctor sets of "before and after" pictures. A man with a useless wrist, unable to manage his boat or help haul a net while the fish were running; then the same man sending his dory across the water with long, strong strokes of the oars, singing lustily. Still more vivid in his memory were two pictures of a little boy: one, a "starved little wretch all tied in knots" from the after-effects of infantile paralysis; two, a straight-limbed lad who went home laughing and shouting. In a moment of discouragement, he liked to recall a little girl running about bouncing a rubber ball. She hardly knew which was the more wonderful— her new leg, cured by an operation, or a ball that bounced into the air, something she had never seen before.

How the rewards accumulated as the years passed! At the Children's Home in St. Anthony, he saw starved, forsaken-looking creatures grow up before his eyes into strong young people; and listless, sober children turn into laughing, rollicking boys and girls. Half-grown youngsters, who couldn't tell one letter from another, went to a Grenfell School and "got learning." He would come upon them later when they had gone back to their own villages. They would be writing letters for "Uncle Billy" or "Aunt Nellie," who had never held pen or pencil between their fingers, or teaching other children to play "Looby Loo" or "All On the Train for Boston."

Everybody likes to play Santa Claus. Few, like the doctor, have a chance to act the part for children who have never heard of Santa Claus before and have never seen a Christmas tree. And just imagine being the person to bring the first Teddy bear ever seen on a whole coast!

"We had an old spruce all ablaze like t'burnin' bush and presents on it for everybody." A boy who spent Christmas in one of the Mission hospitals described the wonderful sight over and over. His eyes were as bright as the Christmas candles.

"Did they like the toys, Tom?" Grenfell asked a fisherman. A box of toys had been sent one Christmas to him and his neighbors.

"Like them, Doctor? Why, they most all had to be beat the same night, 'cos they wouldn't go to bed and leave them."

The doctor smiled, for he knew the so-called "beating" of those children had been gently given. That box of toys had certainly given *him* a lot of fun.

Sometimes Christmas was a convenient excuse for

helping a family without hurting anyone's pride. One day he watched Willie —— buying a few necessities at the trader's store. First, he would look longingly at the warm socks his little girl, Sally, needed so badly to keep her feet warm as she trudged over the snow to school. Then he would eye the slab of oleomargarine on the counter. A little of that would mean a lot to the whole family. Dry bread didn't stick to their ribs long this weather. Which *should* he buy?

Dr. Grenfell could read the fisherman's mind as well as if he had spoken his thoughts. "Willie," he asked casually, as if an idea had just occurred to him, "do you mind helping me choose a Christmas present for Sally? You know I haven't had time to pick out anything for her yet."

"Her could do with the socks."

"Then socks it shall be, and I'll give her two pairs; she'll love to give one pair to her brother."

Willie bought the oleomargarine—a whole pound of it—and started for home on a run. The doctor stood for a moment looking after him and picturing the scene that would follow in a certain cottage when those parcels were unwrapt.

A girl who had been shuffling around in a pair of her father's old shoes, was shod in a pair of her own. Lo! the whole expression of her face and her carriage were changed. A boy, ashamed to go to school because his flour-sack trousers bore plainly inscribed on the seat,

"Pillsbury's Best," started proudly on a run to show off to schoolmates the new pair received from the Mission. The sight of that girl and that boy was a big fee.

So was the warmhearted hospitality the doctor received all along the coast. One couple insisted on getting out of their beds in the middle of a cold winter's night and making the floor their bed so that he might be comfortable over night. Families who were reduced to a diet of flour and water for themselves would keep a little hoard of cocoa and tinned milk on hand specially for Dr. Grenfell's visits. When he wanted to pay for food and lodging, the Labrador liveyere would shake his head emphatically. "It's the way o' t'coast," said he.

If people talked to Dr. Grenfell about his "life of self-sacrifice," he was puzzled. "I've never been conscious of making any sacrifices," was his answer. He considered himself highly paid for everything he ever did, and could say with the Greek poet, Euripides, "Silver and gold are not the only coin."

CHAPTER TWELVE

A Hospital in Record Time

There was a great deal going on in the woods near St. Anthony. By day, the thud-thud of axes, the sharp reports made by falling trees, the harsh singing of crosscut saws, and the voices of men were like instruments in a great orchestra. By night, the dogs reverted to type and howled like wolves. A hundred men and three hundred huskies were camping out there atop six feet of snow in the early spring of nineteen hundred.

How they worked—those hundred men! No one worked harder than Dr. Grenfell. He was in charge of the commissary, and all the food eaten by this army of ravenous men and dogs had to be hauled from St. Anthony on dogsleds. At the start he hadn't quite realized what he was in for, not until the woodcutters ate up in one day his first load of food, which he had expected would last for two weeks. Then it was swiftly borne in upon him that most of his time for the next two weeks would be spent in driving a dog team.

Of course nothing could have suited him better at a time of year when navigating a boat was out of the question. Next to sailing, there was no kind of travel for Wilfred Grenfell like gliding over the snow and ice behind a lively team of dogs. Others could sit back in their armchairs on deluxe trains. Others could have expensive motorcars. Give him a komatik and some strong huskies every time.

What a fortnight that was he spent with the men of St. Anthony on such a camping trip as he had never known before! They were snug and cosy in the snowy woods, sleeping in tilts on balsam beds, mingling their work with songs and stories, eating meals that tasted simply delicious—chunks of fried salt pork and boiled "doughboys" washed down with partridge or ptarmigan soup. It was food to stick to a man's ribs through long, strenuous hours in the frosty outdoors and keep him warm. The kitchen where they cooked the meals was a pleasant place, a great room dug out of the snow clear down to the ground, screened by thick spruce trees and warmed by a roaring fire.

To play Indian like this in northern woods delighted the part of Grenfell that had never grown up. No boy liked a good tussle with wind and cold and snow better than he did. It was a game. So was camp life. He enjoyed tremendously the give and take with these plain men of the woods and the sea.

Even if he had not loved the life of woodsman and

sled driver, he would still have sung for happiness. The trees that were toppling over and being sawed into boards were materials for a new hospital in St. Anthony. No more performing operations in a "glorified cupboard," as he called the little room where he lived and worked as best he could that winter.

What a satisfaction to watch that pile of lumber growing! Before the autumn came, trees now standing would be part of a new building thirty-six feet by thirty-six feet. A hospital in six months! Was ever one raised in so short a time before? To be sure, it was built of green timber and would warp and develop all sorts of cracks and kinks. Yet this building had to be put up quickly or not at all. The wood must be hauled while there was firm snow to draw it on, and most of the work must be done before open water. Then the fish would be striking in and no man on the coast would have even a minute for anything except catching, drying, and salting cod.

When the days in the woods were over, there was a new kind of music, played by hammers and saws and lathes and planes, on the shores of the harbor. All this bustle and noise had been set in motion by the doctor.

"Come and spend a winter with us; we need you just as much as they do in Labrador."

"Start a hospital here if you possibly can."

"My family and I are starving."

Messages such as these had brought Dr. Grenfell to

Sir Wilfred Grenfell

the village of St. Anthony in the fall of eighteen hundred ninety-nine, after the Indian Harbor Hospital had been closed for the winter. There was no doubt about their needing a doctor here and in all the villages hereabouts. It didn't take Grenfell more than a day to realize that. People living on this northern coast of Newfoundland suffered from the same living conditions, the same isolation, and just as many neglected ills as did the Labrador liveyeres.

So he had hired a room in a trader's cottage and gone to work. From village to village, the news was borne as if by some rider on a magic carpet right out of *"Arabian Nights."* The sick did not wait for the doctor to come to them. They fairly invaded St. Anthony, putting up in crowded fishermen's cottages while he treated them.

Singlehanded Dr. Grenfell toiled through short winter days and far into the long winter nights, sometimes in his own small room, sometimes in a cottage kitchen. Emergency operations were performed and broken bones were set on kitchen tables by the pale light of kerosene lamps. It was a repetition of that first summer down North. To make any noticeable impression on all the ills that needed care, he would have had to have a hospital, an assistant, and a staff of nurses. Finally he did enlist the help of a trustworthy woman, gave her some instruction in nursing, and turned over a little of the almost overwhelming burden to her.

In some ways, this first winter Dr. Grenfell spent in

112

the North was "one long delight." The feeling of being shut away from the outside world appealed to the explorer in him. So did the bite of that cruel cold blown by the wind till it scourged the body. There was time to get acquainted with the men and their families at this season of leisure and long evenings by the stove. He wouldn't have missed those months for anything.

Yet it was a baffling, agonizing winter, too. People came to him who needed surgery too delicate and too complicated to be performed on kitchen tables. He was called to the bedsides of those who were dying for want of good nursing. "There's no use," he finally told the men of St. Anthony, "I can't carry on here another winter without a hospital."

The fishermen were undaunted. "We'll build one," they said, "and we'll start now." So they harnessed their dogs and cracked their whips.

This was how it came about that in the fall of that year a hospital stood on the shores of St. Anthony ready for Dr. Grenfell. 'Twas painted yellow with brown trimming, and over the door was written in large letters:

"Faith, Hope, and Love Abide
But the Greatest of These is Love."

Scarcely was the building finished when a furnace dropped right out of the skies. At least the gift was just as unexpected as though the gray winter sky had actually opened. A message came from the Government Engineer of Newfoundland: he offered to provide both the furnace and the necessary piping to heat the homemade hospital. A furnace here in this little fishing village! What wouldn't that mean to the sick! Dr. Grenfell didn't know when he had been quite so pleased about anything.

"But where would you put a furnace?" asked someone of a practical turn of mind. "There's no cellar, and the building sits right on solid rock."

"We'll have to blast a place out of the rock for it," said Grenfell.

Then a hunt began for dynamite. There was some at Flowers Cove, he learned, about sixty miles away by dogsled. Harnessing his team, he started off. Back he came in a few days, with a case of dynamite tied onto the sled, sitting cheerfully astride the explosive load, as if it were a sack of potatoes.

No wonder people thought that the Lord took special care of the doctor.

When the gift from the Government Engineer arrived from St. John's, a cellar was ready for it, and one can be sure that no time was lost in installing that furnace. How proud St. Anthony was of their hospital built by themselves—and heated with a furnace! And certainly it was the pride of Dr. Grenfell. The little building had a long and useful life. It lasted for twenty-five years—

with some alterations and additions—and saved nobody knows how many lives.

To the doctor, the plain wooden building stood for many things—for the spirit of the men of St. Anthony, for as merry a piece of cooperation as he had ever taken part in, for the first of a number of buildings that rose in that Newfoundland village one after another as time went on, till it became the headquarters of the Mission. He had only to look at the hospital to hear again the sound of axes and saws and the voices of a hundred men, the soughing of pines and spruces in the March wind, and the howling of three hundred dogs under the stars.

CHAPTER THIRTEEN

This Took Courage

One fall, when Dr. Grenfell was starting south for a winter of lecturing and money-raising, he put in at Red Bay, a small village on the Straits of Belle Isle. There, on the fishing stage, sat as forlorn a little group of men as he had ever seen, with boxes and newspaper-wrapped bundles, like hoboes off on a trip.

"Doctor," they begged, "us can't stay here this winter and keep alive. Us can't." It had been a bad season. These men had not earned enough to give them even a next-to-starvation diet through the winter.

It was the same old problem—poverty. He had done so little to cure that. Again and again a voice within him had cried out the reproach: *"They ask for bread and you give them—medicine."* Sometimes patients were so poor the doctor wondered if it were a kindness or a wrong he did them in adding to their time on earth.

Well, what was to be done now for this little band of desperate ones begging like children to be taken

Logging for the hospital

away? He certainly couldn't just pack them into his boat and steam off. If only it were as simple as that!

Should he do what he had wanted to do for some time—start a cooperative store on this coast, run by the fishermen, like those cooperatives in England and Scotland? Had he the courage?

"Don't get the traders down on you," his friends had warned him. "Stick to your doctoring and don't put your nose into things that are none of your business."

None of his business! What, then, was he here for? Just to keep people able to drag one foot after another and pull a net out of the sea? Louder than any such warning was that voice within him repeating: *"They ask for bread and you give them—medicine."*

"Starvation coast" was a good name for Labrador, but the coast wasn't to blame. The biggest reason for starvation here was the "truck system" of doing business, which made the men who hauled the nets practically slaves. This was the way it worked: The traders advanced money for the nets, the salt, or other equipment the fisherman needed. In return the fisherman agreed to turn over his catch. Out of the money the fish brought in, the trader took the amount owed to him. The rest—what there was left—was paid as a rule in groceries or other goods at prices set by the trader.

'Twas an easy-going hit-or-miss arrangement, a left-over from days of dealing with Indians and Eskimos, who could not even speak English. It gave a dishonest trader every chance to be dishonest and encouraged an irresponsible or unlucky fisherman to run up debts. Many lived all their lives in debt and died in debt.

He would try showing this north coast a new way of doing business—*right now*. Oh yes, he remembered what cautious friends had said, "You'll burn your fingers if you start cooperatives here." Burn his fingers— he'd do worse than that! There were reefs and breakers and icebergs ahead, he well knew. The traders would fight him. And the fishermen might turn out to be their own worst enemies. They were used to credit, used to letting the trader take all the risks. Would they stick to a cash business? Would they stand on their own feet?

Today they were desperate enough to try anything, thought the doctor. So was he.

"We'll have a meeting tonight of the village and all the families who live anywhere near," he told them, "and then we'll see what can be done."

That evening a story was told that had never been heard in Labrador before. It was the story of how enterprising men and women in England had organized stores of their own called "cooperatives," run by themselves. To start such a store, the people must be willing to put their own money into it—one could become a member by buying even one five-dollar share. Then they must pay cash for everything they bought. Easy credit was enormously expensive in the long run, the doctor told them. It always meant high prices. Also they would have to attend shareholders' meetings and give time and thought to the enterprise. What about it? Did they want to start a cooperative store here in Red Bay?

They were interested, but frightened.

"Will it have to be called a store?" they asked.

"If us buys shares, will us have to sign our names to anything?"

Fearfully, unwilling that the traders should know what was being done or who was doing it, the men of Red Bay and of the coast thereabouts literally emptied their stockings to start a cooperative store. The entire savings of seventeen families totaled eighty-five dollars. The rest of the money needed came out of the doctor's own pocket.

That daring venture, started by desperate men, was a success for a number of years. It kept hunger from Red Bay and freed those seventeen families from debt. It was followed by other cooperative ventures.

Never did Dr. Grenfell forget, so long as he lived, the stormy all-night meeting that launched one of these cooperatives a few miles from St. Anthony. For weeks he had fairly talked himself hoarse to the fishermen, explaining how a cooperative was run and telling what the people of Red Bay had done for themselves. Still the men were afraid to set up a store of their own. Just to talk about it made them feel like plotters. They whispered and looked over their shoulders. If Dr. Grenfell had suggested going down to St. John's and blowing up Government House, they could hardly have felt more guilty. Finally a goodly number of men in that region agreed to turn out for a meeting in a village fourteen miles from St. Anthony.

The evening came. Faced with making a stand openly for what they called "the copper store," some got cold feet. "As 'tis now, the traders has to feed we," they said. A minister who had been an enthusiastic backer of co-operation sent his regrets at the last minute: he had to go to a village twenty miles in the opposite direction to hold a service, he said.

"Um-m-m-m! A service twenty miles away on this particular evening." Dr. Grenfell proceeded to do a little detective work and learned that a certain trader had offered this enthusiast for cooperation a team of dogs to take him *away* from the meeting.

"Suppose—just suppose—the driver of the team should lose his way and go right around in a circle," he said smiling to himself. "Nothing is easier, on these pathless white wastes." Hunting up the man who was to do the driving, he had a confidential talk with him.

There! At last he was off with his own dog team and driver. He chuckled. How surprised that minister would be when he found himself at the meeting! Jim and Pete and George and a few others had been talked out of their fears. It was certainly a wonder he wasn't chilly, after warming so many cold feet. He mustn't be late.

That would give the traders too much time to talk the plan down beforehand. "Take the short cut across the bay," he told the driver.

Crack! Crack! The ice was not equal to the load. The doctor was plunged into a bath of ice-cold sea water. "Throw me the end of the whip," he called to the driver, who had been running alongside the komatik and had not broken through. "Easy now."

Lying flat on his stomach, the man inched toward the black hole into which dogs, sled, and passenger had fallen. When he was near enough, he gave the tough walrus-hide whip a flick as if he were casting for a fish. He caught a big one. Slowly he hauled the dripping doctor to safety, no worse for the ducking. A plunge into ice water was a common experience for Dr. Grenfell. What bothered him was all this lost time. And now there was nothing to do but stop at a cottage and borrow some dry clothes.

"Look at him. He's dressed up in somebody else's clothes for the meeting," said one of the traders with a laugh, when Dr. Grenfell walked into the little village store clad in a fisherman's blue jersey and overalls. It was just as he expected. The traders of the whole region had turned out and they had been making the most of their time, pouring cold water on the plan.

Did they think he had put on a disguise? Grenfell wondered. The sight of such a solid turnout of men who were there expressly to fight him was disturbing. Perhaps he was reminded of the days when he waged a lone fight against a whole gang of boys to protect Mad G?

The traders had the head start, and—a plan of action! As soon as the meeting had been opened by the doctor with a prayer, up jumped one of them and began to talk. The instant he sat down, up jumped another as if released by a spring. It was like a filibuster, only carried on by many in collusion instead of by one. The hour grew late. Still the fishermen said nary a word. In the first place, they were as scared as rabbits, and in the second place, none of them was quick enough to grab an instant's break in the talk before another trader was launched on a fresh tirade against cooperative stores.

At last, far into the night, one fisherman managed to get in a word or two. It was a telling shot. "What I want to know is this, if this copper store buys a barrel of flour for five dollars a barrel in St. John's, will it sell it to we for ten dollars?"

Good for George! Now perhaps other fishermen would take the floor. Couldn't one of them summon courage to follow up his bold neighbor? No. The rest sat silent like rows of owls. The meeting broke up without any action being taken. The traders had had a wonderful time.

"Why—oh why—did they have to be so timid," lamented Grenfell to himself. "They hadn't even fought one round." He came out into the cold, crisp darkness. There, on the steps and in the yard, another meeting was being held under the stars. The men, so silent while inside, were now chattering like magpies. Even the howling of the dogs that waited impatiently to go home could not drown the sounds of their voices.

"If them traders has so much to say against this copper store, it must be a good t'ing." This, in a few words, was what all the chattering was about. The traders had not won out, after all. The stars grew pale. Still the fishermen talked on. The sky was gray before this second meeting broke up and the dogs were bounding off for home. By that time plans were well under way for the new store.

As time went on, other stores were founded, and a cooperative sawmill. Some of these ventures were successful for a number of years. One store still goes on today. Some failed dismally through mismanagement. It was too big a jump for most of the fishermen to take—a jump from a state of childlike dependence on a trader to a manage-your-own-business-on-a-cash-basis cooperative.

Nothing the doctor ever did in a venturesome life took more courage than this attack on the truck system. Criticism pelted down on his head. He lost friends. The failures were enormously costly, for when he paid the debts, the money came either from his own none-too-well-lined purse or was contributed by personal friends. None of the Mission's funds were used for this purpose.

They were putting it mildly, those who said he would

burn his fingers. The experiment cost money and time and peace of mind beyond reckoning. However, the stores that succeeded proved something important—that desperate poverty need not be the common lot of a Labrador fisherman, if an antiquated system could be abolished and business be carried on for cash and cash only. So completely did he prove this that today the Government of Newfoundland backs cooperatives and pays someone to educate the men along the coast in cooperative methods of doing business.

Was Wilfred Grenfell impractical? Or did he just see something forty years sooner than those around him did?

Twenty-Four Hours on an Icepan

Jack, the little black spaniel, missed not a move his master made. Dr. Grenfell was harnessing the dogs in a terrific hurry. Now he was packing up the sled with blankets, medicine kit, pork buns—how good they smelled—a thermos bottle full of cocoa, whale meat for the dogs, firewood. Hurrah! They were going on a long trip by dogsled.

Crack! went the doctor's long whip like a pistol shot. "Haul up, Brin," he called to the brindled leader of the team, "come on, Jack" to the spaniel. They were off for a cottage sixty miles away on the other side of Hare Bay. This was the pleasantest thing ever a little dog could do, thought Jack—to run fast as the wind over the snow until he was tired, then to curl up in a ball on the komatik. "Hurry!" he barked to the team.

The air was like crystal and the landscape was sparkling white and clear blue. Yet this morning Dr. Grenfell scarcely saw the shining day, or felt the tingle of the bracing air. Two men with a team of dogs had come dashing into the village of St. Anthony with the message, "Come at once!" He was racing with time for a sick boy's life, and his thoughts were all concentrated on winning that race.

It was Easter Sunday, and Easter was late that year of 1908. Yet there were no signs of spring in Northern Newfoundland. The harbor was still ice-locked. Fox Farm Hill and all the other hills round about were white. The only way to get to the other side of the Bay was the long way around by land.

The dogs were strong and fresh. They needed little urging, even if Jack did pretend they were slowpokes, and soon the tired team that had come for the doctor was left behind. By the time twilight was blurring the shore line, twenty miles of the journey had been covered—a good afternoon's run for huskies.

That night the doctor, who was usually a sound sleeper, kept waking up and listening. Disturbing sounds came through the cracks in the walls of the cottage where he spent the night. Not the howling of the huskies —they were always making the night hideous with their voices, and Dr. Grenfell had long since learned to sleep through that doleful sound. It was the wind. It had changed direction and was driving mist and fog in from the sea. That meant soft snow tomorrow, slow traveling tomorrow. And what a heavy sea! The ice was breaking up out there, with rumblings and loud reports, piling up "ballicaters," great barricades of ice, all along the shore. That meant there would be no such thing as slipping quickly along over the ice. Well, they'd have to make a crack-o'dawn start.

Before the sky was even gray, lanterns were gleaming inside and outside the cottage. Dogs were being harnessed. The doctor ate his breakfast of pork buns, which were biscuits with little pieces of pork in them, and washed them down with cocoa. Jack swallowed his bun almost whole. "You go ahead and I'll catch up with you at the log tilt across the bay," he told the driver of the other team. Since his huskies were so much faster than theirs, he was giving the two messengers a two-hour start.

By the time the second team was starting, rain was falling. Soft snow, ballicaters, and now rain! "Haul up, Brin. Come on, Jack. We'll get there somehow."

Wait a minute. There was a small island out in the bay and a bridge of ice reaching to it. From that island to the other side was only four miles. Could he make it? To be sure there *were* some great cracks in the ice. Still it looked fairly strong. A boy's life might be the price of going cautiously around. "Urra!" he called, and Brin turned sharp left. So far, so good. They were on the island. The doctor peered ahead again. The ice out there was rough; it had been broken up by the waves and then packed together by the wind. Should he risk it? He thought of the boy and of the boy's father and mother waiting and watching for him. "Haul on, Brin! Come, Jack."

The rocky point four miles ahead that loomed just above Brin's ears drew nearer and nearer. Now it couldn't be more than two miles away, now a mile. The last mile dwindled under the gliding runners. Ah! only a quarter of a mile more. "Haul on, Brin."

Why! What had become of that wind? The wind that had been pushing the masses of ice together? It was blowing out to sea. All at once the whole mass they were on began to loosen and separate into icepans. Perhaps he'd better go back. He turned around. Behind him were only floating pans separated by great black gaps of open water. There was *no* turning back now. There would be no going forward in a few moments. Go it, Brin! Go it, Doc, and Moody, and Jerry! Go it, Sue, and Watch, and Spy! Run for your lives. Run for your master's life. Run as you never ran before!

Pulling on his oilskins, Grenfell threw himself on his hands and knees beside the sled, so as to spread the weight of the load over a wider space. All the time he was urging the dogs forward. Oh, Brin! Don't hesitate like that. Haul on! Haul on! Why *couldn't* the brindled dog understand?

Too late! One instant's hesitation had spelled disaster. The sled began to sink. The dogs had to pull twice as hard as before. Then they began to sink. Suddenly the dogs and master were all in the icy, slushy water.

Quickly Grenfell cut the traces of the harness so as not to be pulled down by the floundering huskies. Only the leader's trace he kept—wound tight around his wrist. Wasn't there an icepan they could climb onto? Good for Brin! He had found a one—a very small one. Hand over hand, the doctor pulled himself by the trace toward the leader and at least a few moments' safety. Almost there now. Just a moment more. Then Brin, as if possessed by an evil spirit, slipped out of his harness and left his master stranded in the water.

Everything began to be more and more of an effort the longer he stayed in the ice-cold water. How drowsy he was beginning to feel! He mustn't give in to that feeling. He'd freeze to death if he did. Grabbing hold of the trace from another dog's harness, he began again struggling desperately toward the floating bit of ice. Slowly and with difficulty he pulled himself up beside the leader. The rest of the dogs followed. Master and dogs huddled close together to keep from falling off the small ice raft.

What to do next? The doctor took stock of his situation. The icepan was being pushed all the time further from shore. It would break up in almost no time in open water. Gone were his coat, cap, gloves, and oilskins. Behind him on the half-sunk sled, lay thermos bottle, warm blankets, wood—everything he needed to keep from freezing. He *must* find a larger icepan. There, about twenty yards away, was one that looked fairly substantial. He'd make a try to get there. Splicing the traces of Brin and Doc, the two leaders, he tied them to himself. Would they pull him across?

He urged them. He shouted at them. Again and again he pointed to the larger pan. No. They were not going. They would not leave this bit of ice. He seized the struggling resisting animals and threw them into the water. Back they climbed. Again he pushed them off, and again. Each time they climbed back beside him. Their master had always been kind to them before, but today he was trying to drown them. That was the way it looked to the dogs.

What should he do? Desperately, Dr. Grenfell tried to think of some way to make his team understand what he was trying to tell them. Jack, the little spaniel, looked up into his face and wagged a plumy tail, as if to ask, "Can I help?" Many a time in the past Jack, by dashing along ahead of the dog team, had sped them on when they had begun to slow down. There was no fear in his brown eyes. In fact he couldn't quite understand what was the trouble. Light as a scrap of fluff, he could walk anywhere on the thin surface ice.

"Yes, Jack. Perhaps you're the very one who can help. See that pan out there? I'll throw this little piece of ice on it. There. Go after it!"

Off dashed the spaniel, as readily as if he were chasing a stick in his own dooryard. Presently a little black spot lay in the middle of the icepan. Brin and Doc eyed the spaniel, as if to say, "Oh! that's where he wants us to go." Then, Splash! They had jumped in and started swimming toward Jack. The doctor followed. The other dogs, now on the loose, floundered after them and all but one reached the goal safely. The little black dog welcomed them, proud as Punch over having led the way.

Grenfell saw at once that this pan was anything but safe. It was larger than the other, but they were still on sish ice—small bits ground off icepans held together by a thin coating of surface ice. The wind was bitter and blew offshore. They were drifting back the way they had worked so hard to come. And nobody would think of looking for the doctor in the middle of Hare Bay. Even if a fisherman saw black specks out here, he'd take them for seals. As for the men who had gone ahead, by the time they missed him and came all the way back, well, he'd be either frozen or drowned. Better not think ahead! Just do the next thing. Right now the next thing was to do something about his back. The wind drove right through his flannel shirt. His eye fell on his long sealskin boots. He had taken them off to empty the water and ice out of them. Slitting them up with his hunting knife, he tied the pieces of skin to his shoulders and back, making a windbreaker. There. That was better. His fingers weren't quite so numb either, since he'd been using them.

Slowly, but surely, the pan floated seaward with its

load. In a short time it was drifting past the island. Back there again, after all this struggle! Now the bridge of ice to the opposite shore was gone. There was no chance of getting to land. In spite of the sealskin windbreaker, the cold seemed to penetrate to the doctor's very marrow. The old flannel football suit he wore—a relic of Oxford days—was like mosquito netting in this icy blast.

"I've got to do it! That's all. I've got to have their skins, or I'll be frozen stark within the hour." A look of grim desperation was in his face.

Quickly and mercifully he killed three of the dogs. It was the hardest thing he had ever done. Those huskies were almost members of his family. He skinned them at once and wrapped himself in their deep-furred coats. What grateful warmth! No wonder a Labrador dog could stand any degree of cold without freezing so much as a toe.

Now, what could he do about his feet? They were losing all feeling. Cutting pieces of rope from the dogs' harnesses, he unraveled the fibre and stuffed it into his wet moccasins. At least it was dry. He wouldn't freeze for a while anyway. Gradually the dusk crept out from the land mercifully blurring the sight of that black open sea and the ever-narrowing distance between the pan and destruction out there in the choppy water.

A light gleamed from a fisherman's cottage on the shore of the Bay. It was a tantalizing reminder of warmth and shelter. If only there was some way of letting those

The doctor falls into the bay

people over there know the plight he was in. A fire might do it, but he had no wood. Perhaps he could make some of that raveled rope burn by soaking it in fat from the dog's carcasses. He pulled out the box of matches he always wore chained to himself, so they never could be lost. Every single match in the box was soaking wet. The stars came out overhead. He longed to pull one down and set it on the pan for a great beacon light.

There was nothing more he could do—except wait. Where would another morning's light find him? He wasn't afraid to die. Death, he felt sure, was just a passing from one life into another. It was leaving this work he minded. That was what kept him, fighting, fighting to stay alive. For sixteen years he had been working among these fishermen. Could it be as long as that since the morning in 1892 when he had first looked on these rocky shores? Why, he had only just begun to carry out the long, long plans in his mind for Labrador.

It was not a record to be ashamed of, the record of those years. He was proud of his four hospitals. And there was his floating hospital, the *Strathcona*. How many men, women, and children had found relief from pain in her cabin? He couldn't begin to count them. The Children's Home—he liked to think of the boys and girls there. Yet these things and everything else he had done seemed so little, when put alongside his plans and dreams. He needed twenty—no, forty years. Oh, at least forty years to work for Labrador!

Next year he would double the size of two buildings at St. Anthony—the hospital and the Children's Home. Then there were those boarding schools he wanted to start. A Seamen's Institute in St. John's—that dream must come true. The rug-making and other home industries, there were wonderful future possibilities for them. A chain of lighthouses along that perilous Labrador shore, a telegraph, model farms and greenhouses, more cooperatives—there was no end to the doctor's plans. More time, he *must* have more time.

All at once the lines of an old hymn sung themselves in his ears:

> "My God, my Father, while I stray
> Far from my home on life's rough way,
> Oh, help me from my heart to say,
> Thy will be done."

It wasn't for him to say whether or not his work on this coast were done. If his time had come, he'd have to go. But how he hoped there'd be lots of work to do in the next world, and boats. Let there be boats in heaven!

Cuddling close to the largest dog for warmth, and with Jack in a contented ball for a foot-warmer, the doctor fell asleep.

"Git your spyglasses and come quick."
George Read jumped up from the supper table, threw

on a coat, grabbed his heavy, antiquated binoculars and
a cap and was on the way to the headland with George
Davis in practically no time at all. He was used to being
summoned quickly at this time of year, when everybody
was watching out for seals. Yet there was something in
his neighbor's manner that made him anxious to be off.

They ran without speaking in their haste to beat the
darkness. "Yonder! What is it?" Davis pointed to a pan
some three miles away. Read adjusted the binoculars and
looked in the direction the finger pointed. "Looks—like
—a—man. 'Tis a man! 'E's moving! There's dogs, too."

Each looked into the other's face, as if unwilling to
speak his thoughts. Not the doctor! Oh, not *the doctor!*
Yet it couldn't be anybody else. Who else on the coast
took such chances as he did to get to his patients? These
were the things they were thinking. They went and told
George Andrews what they had seen.

If only it were possible to put right out in a boat!
Why couldn't they have discovered him earlier? To try
to make their way in that floating ice with a heavy sea
would be dangerous even in daylight. With darkness
coming on, it would be suicide. Dr. Grenfell had risked
his life again and again for others. Now he was in danger, and they were powerless to save him. "I'll go after
him as soon as it's light, no matter what chances I take,"
vowed George Andrews. The other two had the same
resolve. There was little or no sleep for the fishermen
in the cottages along Hare Bay that night.

The doctor woke himself shivering. Where was he? Still on the pan, and the pan was considerably nearer the sea—a restless, white-toothed sea.

With startling suddenness the wind died down. Would this last? Or was the lull just a preparation for a harder blow? The calm continued. The doctor fell asleep again.

When he woke the next time, he had a plan of action. His mind had apparently been working on the problem while he slept. "You're not a dead man yet," he told himself. "Rig up a flag and begin waving it as soon as daylight comes. If folks on shore see something moving out here, they'll know at least that some kind of animal is on this pan."

Of all the flags ever contrived the one Dr. Grenfell hoisted just before dawn that day was the weirdest. The staff was made of the leg bones from the carcasses, tied together with bits of harness, and the flag was the football shirt. At the first crack of dawn, he raised the shaky banner high—as high as he could—and waved the crooked staff till his arms ached. For hour after hour he kept on waving. The sun came up. Still the strangely-clad figure stood upholding a crooked standard that flew a flannel shirt.

Were those men over on the cliffs? No. Only trees. Was that a boat bobbing up and down in the sun? No. Just another icepan.

" 'E's alive! 'E *is!* See 'e's wavin' to we." The sight was worth the struggle the fishermen had been making ever since daylight. All the while they were risking their lives, pushing their boat between grinding icepans and hauling it over stretches of sish ice, they had fully expected to find the doctor dead. It seemed a miracle that he had lived through the long night in the bitter cold. When they reached the frail piece of ice that held him up, they were sure that a miracle had saved him.

"Didn't seem like 'twas the doctor. Looked so old and 'is face a queer color," Andrews said when he told the story afterward. They grasped his hands, but he could not return the warm clasp. His hands were like chunks of wood; they were frozen. He had to be helped into the boat, so badly frozen were his feet. Not till they had given him a few swallows of hot tea from the bottle they had brought with them, could he speak. His first words were that he was sorry, terribly sorry to have caused them all this trouble.

Trouble! After all the chances he took and the hardships he endured to help them in their hours of need. At his words, tears came into their eyes.

The doctor's next thought was of the sick boy. Yet he could not be of any help to him now. There was only one thing to do—go home. Back to St. Anthony he went, "hauled like a log," as he put it. For the next few days he lay a patient in his own hospital, cared for by a thankful staff that had never expected to see him alive again.

The black spaniel couldn't make out why his everactive master was in bed. "You saved my life, Jack," the doctor told him, "when you weren't afraid to jump off that piece of ice and lead the way for the team." Did the little silky dog understand? Or did he wonder why in the world everyone was suddenly making such a fuss over him?

As soon as he could write, Dr. Grenfell sent off the following letter, making light of the narrow escape, as a man would to an elderly mother—

"Dearest Mum:

"You will hear, I suppose, I had an accident on the ice and fell through. I think nothing of that because I know exactly how to get out, having been in so often. But I could not get ashore, and had a night out, drifting about on a rather small piece of ice. I can hear you say 'how horrible'! Not at all. It proved a most valuable experience. Of course, being wet through and having lost my clothing and komatik, I had to get some more. What do you think I did? I had one of Uncle Joe's long knives. I killed three of my dogs. (I had eight with me.) I skinned them and made a Robinson Crusoe coat. I had only football things, my old Oxford ones, as I was running fast and it is hot in spring. I do wish you could have seen me come ashore next morning. I was comfortable enough to sleep well, tossed about in a good breeze of wind upon the ice. I had the black spaniel you sent as a hot water bottle for my toes!! And I cuddled up round my largest eskimaux dog. He was as hot as can be. I couldn't help laughing because he was so snug. He had the cheek to growl when I moved. Fancy it— In the morning he stretched and yawned and gave me a kiss, and then went off to sleep again. Please don't get nervous over the affair. God taught me a wonderful lesson, and I wouldn't not have gone through it for worlds. It will help me all through life, I know, and so I hope help others. I hurt my toes and fingers a little, but never found that out till I got home. It does us all good to have a fair and square look into death's face. It makes the things of earth so much less important except as tools to use for Christ.

"Ever your absolutely well and perfectly happy son,

W. T. G."

The men who came through heavy seas and ice to Dr. Grenfell's rescue received presents of spyglasses and watches inscribed, "In memory of April 21st." How they treasured those gifts! Yet, as they told the doctor, they didn't need anything to make them remember that day when they had so nearly lost him.

From Mostyn House there came a sweater and a pair of woolen stockings knitted by Mrs. Grenfell for George Andrews, because he had led the expedition that rescued her son.

As for the sick boy, he was brought to the hospital a day or two later, when the ice had broken up enough to let a boat cross the bay in safety.

One more debt of gratitude remained to be paid by Dr. Grenfell. That was his debt to the three huskies. In the hall of the house in St. Anthony, where he lived, is a bronze tablet inscribed:

Sir Wilfred Grenfell
To the memory of
Three noble dogs
Moody
Watch
Spy
Whose lives were given
For mine on the ice
April 21st, 1908.

CHAPTER FIFTEEN

"The Doctor's Getting Married"

Nothing like this, nothing that made such a stir all along the coast, had ever happened in St. Anthony before. There had been new houses, but none with a glassed-in porch and a big fireplace like the one being built on the hillside, and certainly none with furniture sent all the way from Chicago, off out west somewhere in the States. And what a "wonnerful lot of stuff" the mailboat had put off here—boxes, barrels, chairs and tables and beds in crates, and rolls of carpeting—all for one house.

There had been plenty of newlyweds here before, but this couple was different. Dr. Grenfell was getting married. For seventeen years, the people of Northern Newfoundland and Labrador had felt that he almost belonged to them. Even when he was back home in England or on those long lecture trips, he was working for them, planning to come back down North with more equipment and more funds. Was everything going to be different now? They wondered.

141

What was she like—this American woman he was bringing down here? Was she pretty and would she take good care of the doctor? the women and girls asked.

Would she fit in here or would she be restless and discontented and finally talk the doctor into going away and leaving them, perhaps back to the States? The men discussed this question over and over and from every angle, as they smoked their pipes and warmed themselves by the kitchen stove or at the store. It was winter, and fishermen have plenty of time to smoke and talk in winter.

"T'doctor wouldn't let no woman take 'im away from t'coast."

"You doant never know what a strange woman will do."

"How's a man to know what a woman's like in four days?"

The story of Dr. Grenfell's whirlwind courtship had traveled from village to village. It was more like a story out of a book than something that had actually happened to a busy doctor. Coming back from England that spring of 1909, he had met an American girl just out of Bryn Mawr College. "The handsomest girl on the ship," she was called. So she certainly seemed to Dr. Grenfell. He liked her eyes—sea-blue with dark brows and lashes—and her clear, level glance. He liked her tallness and the way she walked, so erect and as if she meant to get somewhere. She had what Americans called "go."

Yet it wasn't her looks alone that caused him to prefer Anne—he did not know what her last name was—to everyone else on the big Cunarder. It was more fun to walk the deck, play games, drink afternoon tea, or do nothing at all with her, more fun than he'd ever had before.

By the third day out, Grenfell began to dread the end of the voyage. Dread turned into desperation, when the captain announced with pride, "We'll dock in New York day after tomorrow." This new-found companionship, different from any he had ever known before, *mustn't* end day after tomorrow. It mustn't *ever* end. Yet Labrador and Chicago were so far from each other. He and Anne would never meet again, unless—

If only there were some way to slow down this ocean greyhound, as they called her. For once, Wilfred Grenfell was selfish, selfish enough to wish for headwinds, even a storm. Also he was actually glad that his well-loved mother, who was crossing with him for the first time, was forced to stay in her cabin. Watching the *Mauretania's* prow cutting through the water so swiftly and easily was torture. Time! Just a little more time was all he needed.

The ship, proudly hurrying to her goal, would give him no more time. Well, the only thing to do was to beat the liner in. Anyway he was always at his best on the high seas. Just the feel of a rolling deck under his feet gave him courage. So, before the towers of New

York City's skyline had risen out of the mist, the doctor took a deep breath of salt air and proposed to a girl he had never seen four days ago.

She promptly reminded him that he didn't so much as know her name—her last name. Quickly he retorted that he was interested only in what her name was going to be. She didn't say "Yes" and she didn't say "No," but she did invite the doctor and his mother to visit her and her mother at their summer home in Lake Forest, Illinois. There, several weeks later, she did say "Yes," and even decided on the important day—November 18th.

The newspaper reporters, who covered the wedding in Chicago of Anne Elizabeth Caldwell MacClanahan and Wilfred Thomason Grenfell, asked a great many questions. Did she really expect to *live* in Labrador? they quizzed the bride. Why not? Didn't a wife usually make her home where her husband's work was? They reminded Dr. Grenfell of how he had almost lost his life on an icepan the year before. "I suppose you won't be taking such chances now that you're getting married," said one. "My dear sir," was the somewhat indignant reply, "I must get to my patients."

How relieved the fishermen down North would have been if they had heard these interviews!

A Toronto newspaper, however, was distinctly pessimistic. Having listed all the services Dr. Grenfell performed and all the enterprises he ran in the North, the writer ended the account on a dubious note—"And when he is not busy, he will be at home with his wife."

At last the January day came, when the couple, after a honeymoon in the States, sailed into St. Anthony harbor. The whole village trooped down to the landing when they saw the mailboat coming up the long harbor. "Look at the *Prospero!*" they shouted. From the top of her mainmast to the waterline, she was frosted with snow and ice. For nine days—nearly twice as long as the voyage from St. John's usually took—she had been steaming through a blizzard, battling wind, snow, and sleet.

What a terrible first impression the "doctor's woman" would have of the coast, thought the people of St. Anthony. Probably she'd been seasick all the way. Would she want to turn right around and go home to mother?

The *Prospero* drew near shore. A tall, erect girl stood at the prow beside the doctor. She was laughing. She seemed to enjoy a northern blizzard. At the sight of her glowing cheeks and sparkling eyes and the doctor's smiles, the men and women waiting on the dock must have breathed sighs of relief. At least, here was no girl who would be running home to mother.

She looked like a Viking's daughter, who had been born in a fiord and had sailed the seas in a roving Norseman's boat. Anne MacClanahan Grenfell didn't seem easy to know like their doctor, but she would share her

husband's liking for adventure and for a life of action.
There was no doubt about that from the moment she
stepped off the boat in a January gale.

What an appropriate wedding present the people of
the coast chose! It was a picture of a fleet of fishing
schooners framed and inscribed, "Inasmuch as ye did it
unto one of the least of these my brethren, ye did it
unto Me."

Laughter rang out in the new house. If ever two people had fun together, the Grenfells did—laughing, playing jokes on each other, turning ordinary tasks into
hilarious games. They gave parties; Anne Grenfell had a
talent for getting up parties. Once she served supper to
fifty-eight people on the sun porch. Sunday night sup-
pers and Sunday night sings in front of a roaring fire in
the living room fireplace were occasions never to be
forgotten by the guests. So were the evenings when the
doctor read aloud, sometimes a highly amusing tale,
again something serious. He had always been full of fun
and given to playing good-natured jokes on people.
Now his sense of humor was more active than ever, and
the twinkle, that used to come and go in his gray eyes,
seemed always lurking beneath the lids ready to flash
out.

Presently, another sound quite different from laughter
rang through the house. It was the clackety-clack of an
ancient typewriter for hours on end. The machine was
broken—most people would have considered it hopeless

—but Anne Grenfell managed to turn off an amazing number of letters in the course of a day. Thus, early in their marriage, she lifted from Dr. Grenfell's shoulders a burden of correspondence that grew heavier and more important to the work with each year.

Gradually this working partner took over one job after another. The orphanage at St. Anthony interested her. Its family of orphaned or neglected little creatures had been picked up by the doctor along the whole coast. What an assortment of boys and girls those were—brown-skinned Eskimos with bright black eyes and children like pink and white flowers, cripples and children who ran like reindeer, sharp-eyed children and children whose eyes were sightless. Even after Anne Grenfell had two boys and a girl of her own, she kept on carrying a large share of the responsibility for running this other family.

Her own children were all born in St. Anthony. They rode behind husky dogs and sailed on fishing schooners before ever they knew there were such things as motor cars and railroad trains. They were given names that honored ancestors on both sides of the family—Wilfred Thomason, Jr., Kinloch Pascoe, and Rosamond Loveday. Their schooldays were spent in three countries—the United States, Canada, and England.

It was her idea to secure scholarships for Labrador boys and girls so that they might go to Canada and to the States and be trained for services at home. They

Sir Wilfred Grenfell

went to business colleges and came back to run cooperative stores. They graduated from hospitals and normal
schools, and returned full-fledged nurses and teachers.
At agricultural colleges they learned how to cope with
farming handicaps on the coast. When a modern concrete hospital was built at St. Anthony in 1927, a local
boy, who had been trained at Pratt Institute in Brook-
lyn, took entire charge of the job, with masons, carpenters, plumbers, and electricians working under him who
had also been sent outside for training. It was the edu-
cational fund started by Mrs. Grenfell and continued
by her efforts that had given these boys their start.

She threw herself heart and soul into the endless task
of raising money for the many-sided work in which she
was now a partner, organizing a bazaar in London or in
New York City, opening shops to market the rugs and
other handicrafts made in Labrador. She persuaded the
artist and the engraver, who were responsible for the
King of England's Christmas card, to do a Christmas
calendar, sold these calendars for the benefit of the Mission and realized eight thousand dollars from that one
enterprise. She did easily and with enjoyment things that
were just plain drudgery for the doctor, such as organizing committees, arranging lecture tours, keeping ac-
counts. Relieved of such painful but necessary duties,
he was able to give more and more time to the kind of
work that seemed like play to him. What a happy arrangement!

Arrival of S.S. Prospero *with the newlyweds*

"The Doctor's Getting Married"

"I couldn't do it without her," Dr. Grenfell said again and again.

She was "willing to leave all the best which the civilized world can offer to share my life . . . on this lonely shore," he wrote of her humbly in his autobiography.

Yes. Anne MacClanahan left behind a good life in Chicago when she married the doctor from Labrador. Yet what a rich experience in living she gained!

CHAPTER SIXTEEN

"Thank You, Doctor Grenfell"

"Thank you, Dr. Grenfell," said the college boys who had spent the summer vacation fighting mosquitoes and black flies, and digging, digging, digging in St. Anthony. Not a cent of pay had they received for opening up a drain six feet deep and a half mile long through rocks and through earth webbed by tough roots. Not even their expenses to Labrador had been paid. Yet here they were in September, thanking the doctor for the summer, grateful for having been allowed to work harder than a chain gang toiled.

"Thank you, Dr. Grenfell," said the young English woman who for ten years directed the largest orphanage on the coast without a cent of pay.

"I've had a wonderful summer," said a young man who had been cooking three meals a day seven days a week for twenty-one workmen all the time he had been in Labrador.

A famous eye specialist, who gave his services for

eighteen summers to the Grenfell Mission, said that the happiest moment of his whole year began each spring when he received from Dr. Grenfell a wire saying, "The winter ice is breaking up. You can start for the coast."

As remarkable as anything Wilfred Grenfell accomplished was the building up of a small army of men and women ready to do any kind of work from ditch digging to decorating a Christmas tree for any number of hours at a stretch, not only without pay but often at their own expense. The "Wops"—short for "without pay"—was the name they gave themselves, these Grenfell volunteers. They came from all over the United States and Canada, from the British Isles, from Australia, from New Zealand.

"Who made this piece of gravel road?"

"The Wops."

"How did you get this fine dam built way up here?"

"Oh, the Wops built it one summer."

"How do you happen to have running water here in Cartwright?"

"The Wops laid a pipe to a spring off over on the other side of that swamp."

"Who are these Wops anyway?"

"They are people of all ages and both sexes who have discovered that nothing is so much fun as work, work done for the sake of helping somebody else."

One can imagine some such conversation carried on between a visitor to the North and Dr. Grenfell.

No visitor ever heard the whole list of services performed by this gallant band of volunteers. It was too long a tale to be told even between dawn and daylight of a long summer's day in Labrador. Anyway the head of that band was far too busy to tell it. Many of the Mission buildings were put up entirely by volunteer carpenters and masons from plans drawn by volunteer architects. They painted them, too, inside and out. The wireless plants at three hospitals were the work of Wops.

A crew of Yale boys sailed all the way from New Haven to St. Anthony one summer in a new motor launch—the gift of a group of Yale students. They were Wops especially after Grenfell's own heart. And how he liked that present! "She is the most perfect thing of her kind I ever saw," he wrote in his log book. "Her engine can drive her six knots, but she sails so well the engine is hardly needed."

The people who worked for Dr. Grenfell showed a devotion to their tasks that is indeed rare. A boy who helped him one summer to build an industrial center worked right along into September.

"Didn't you tell me you had a job for this fall?" the doctor inquired one day.

"Yes, but I've given it up."

"But *why* did you do that?"

"Because I wanted to finish this job."

He was not a rich boy, either.

Once a troop of Boy Scouts volunteered to lay some

water pipes. The foreman looked them over and decided they were tenderfeet. "Better send them picking daisies, Doctor," he advised.

But the doctor had confidence in them. "They can do the job," he said. "Just try them."

A week later the foreman confessed that he was "fairly knocked out" by what they had accomplished. "I wouldn't have believed it was in them to stick to it as they do."

When Grenfell bought the *Strathcona II* at Southampton, his friends said, "You can't expect to hire anybody to sail that little tub across the ocean."

"I don't," was his reply.

He felt perfectly sure that it wouldn't be necessary to pay for the job, and it wasn't. A volunteer crew braved the northern seas in this little steam yacht only eighty-four feet long, said to have been the smallest boat ever to cross the Atlantic under its own power. When they reached St. John's they, too, said, "Thank you, Dr. Grenfell."

Why did they do it? Why did men and women thank Wilfred Grenfell for being allowed to do work in Labrador and Newfoundland without pay—work that they would have been unwilling to do at home for union wages?

Was it the romantic background? That might account for a person's coming once, if he were a young person. Yet the Grenfell volunteers came again and again, and they were of all ages from Boy Scouts to grandfathers. Were they bored with lives of ease at home? A few were bored at home and a few had ease. However, the greater number were keenly interested in life and worked for a living. They were teachers, nurses, engineers, doctors, lawyers, architects, business men and women. They gave up precious vacations after working hard all the year. Some of them had to do all kinds of things to earn money for their boat and train fare. One young woman sold doughnuts to make her summers in Labrador possible. A young man paid his fare by selling pups. A skilled carpenter, who made from twelve to fourteen dollars a day at home, dropped his work and came from Kentucky to teach Labrador men how to make looms.

As for those from homes of wealth, they gave up cruises on yachts and trips abroad to climb aboard a little coastwise steamer and go "down North."

Why did they do it? Well, Dr. Grenfell had an explanation. He believed that people naturally like to "endure hardness." Softness, love of ease and comfort, these were just by-products of wholly unnatural living in what we call "modern civilization." When he talked to a group of college students about life in Labrador, he told them how hard and uncomfortable it was and how plain was the food, and they flocked to sign up for the next boat. Young nurses he told not of the comparatively comfortable work within the Grenfell hospitals. They heard the story of a nurse who took a five-day dogsled trip in zero weather in order to bring a patient to the hospital before it was too late. Did this scare off the nurses? They begged for the chance to do the same thing.

It looks as if Dr. Grenfell were right about hard, heroic tasks being attractive to people who have not "gone soft." He was right, too, in believing that there are always greathearted men and women ready to help others.

One thing the doctor overlooked in explaining the enthusiasm of the Wops—that was the impact of his greatness on others. This unassuming man never suspected that he was great. Yet others felt the quiet power that was in him. He could infect those around him with his love of life, the magic of his enthusiasm, his simple faith. "Down here all work is play," he said, and somehow it became play—even laying water pipes. "Look at these blue-jerseyed Vikings," he said of the Labrador fishermen, and people could fairly see plain men wearing winged helmets and defying storms in high-prowed boats. "This bare, neglected coast is a storehouse of unused wealth waiting to be opened. Its fisheries, its mines, the power of its waterfalls, these things are not half appreciated. And why," he asked, "are not tourists flocking to these shores to feast on the beauty of fiords and mountains and sea, just as they do to the North Cape? Simply because they have never been told about Labrador."

How could anyone help being affected by such enthusiasm?

Above all, Wilfred Grenfell drew people to him because he had found what everyone wants—a way of living that made him happy. A man who has discovered that will be followed to the end of the world. Could he show others how to be happy too? Yes. He could and he did. "Nowhere have I ever seen people so busy and so happy," remarked a visitor to Labrador.

There is an old tale about a sick king, who was told that he would never be well until he had worn the shirt of a happy man. So he searched his whole kingdom. Finally, after many months, a happy man was found. Alas! he was of no help to the king, for he had not a shirt to his name.

Dr. Grenfell may well have been happier than any other man of his time. Yet he never thought of his own comfort and almost ignored material things. If a warm shirt hadn't been a necessity in cold Labrador, the lack of one would never have worried him. He was always giving away his clothes to people he thought needed them more than he did. A hard bed was the least of his worries. He would crawl into his sleeping bag and find sweet repose on a kitchen floor, on top of a chicken coop, or on the ground. Once someone found him sleeping peacefully under a foot of snow, which had blown into his room and drifted across his bed during the night. A dogsled was more to his liking than the sleekest, shiniest motorcar. Pork buns and tea in a fisherman's cottage tasted better to him than terrapin and quail in a New York or London hotel.

Young men and women thanked Dr. Grenfell, because with him they discovered the possibilities of life "down North," the possibilities of life everywhere.

CHAPTER SEVENTEEN

"Us Had Better Ask the Doctor"

"Us had better ask the doctor," said the fishermen of Labrador, when they were up against problems they could not solve. In their eyes, Wilfred Grenfell was "doctor, lawyer, merchant, chief," and just about everything else mortal man can be.

If a couple wanted to get married and there was no preacher within miles, they hailed the *Strathcona* and begged its doctor-skipper to "say a few words over them." So he had to become a Justice of the Peace. They brought their disputes and their law-breakers aboard the boat, as if it were a floating court instead of a hospital. He was even called upon to settle a fishermen's strike. So he had to be appointed a magistrate.

The sentences handed down by Magistrate Grenfell were, to say the least, original. Two women involved in a feud came to him, and this is how he made peace between them. They were told that they had to drink tea together every other Monday for six weeks. Now it's a difficult matter to sit and glare while you sip a cup of tea. Of course they were chatting and gossiping away like the best of friends before the six weeks' sentence had been served. Another idea of his was to make a prisoner his own jailer. Having ordered an offender shut up, only to find that there was no place to lock him into, he put the culprit in an empty cottage saying, "Bill, if you keep yourself shut in, you'll be out and about your business in two weeks. But for every time anybody sees you outside, two more days will be added to your sentence."

Dr. Grenfell married couples, baptized babies, preached sermons, buried the dead, and helped the survivors to carry on. Those who could not read or write brought their letters to this friend of all Labrador to be read and answered. A trapper who found he was being cheated by the local trader would bring foxskins to the doctor and ask him to sell them.

One day when the *Strathcona* was speeding southward in a fair wind, a small fishing boat put out right across her bows. What a pity to have to stop now, with this breeze billowing the sails! Well, it must be an emergency call. The thought of a race to the bedside of someone critically ill gave Dr. Grenfell that sense of exhilaration he always felt at such times.

Yet there was a hint of regret in his voice as he gave the order "Down sail!"

"Heave to!"

An old man sat at the tiller of the smaller boat. He

climbed slowly and with maddening deliberation over the rail of the hospital ship.

"What's wrong?" asked the doctor, trying hard to keep out of his voice the annoyance he felt at so much delay. "We're in a hurry this morning."

There was no such thing as hurrying this visitor. He was a little like the "aged man a-sitting on a gate . . . whose look was mild, whose speech was slow, whose hair was whiter than the snow." Very slowly he removed his cap and bowed. Very slowly he spoke, "Doc-tor—have—you—got—any—books—to—lend?"

"Books!" So he had dropped sails on a day like this for a man who just wanted something to read!

"There isn't anything to read here," the old man went on, waving his arm toward the shore. "I've got two books, but I've read them over and over."

"What are they?" Dr. Grenfell found himself growing interested in this man who had cut across his bows for a book.

"The *Works of Josephus* and *Plutarch's Lives.*"

Stifling a gasp of utter amazement, the doctor went below to his cabin for some books. How could he feel annoyed! This lover of the classics, who knew Josephus and Plutarch by heart, was starving for mental food. Fortunately the *Strathcona* had a few traveling libraries, boxed and ready to turn over to a school here or a group there who "wanted a bit o' readin'." The old man should have a whole box of books.

"All these, doctor? For me?" What joy was in the faded eyes! Now he was actually in a hurry to get back to his cottage and begin reading. In half the time it had taken him to climb up, he was over the rail. His small boat, with its brown sail filled, skittered back to shore as if it shared the owner's eagerness to be home again.

"Up sails!" On his way went the doctor, making a note in his log that he must get more box libraries. Heaven forbid that he should ever have to refuse a request like this one!

Certainly the emergency cases down North were not always sick people. Percy was one, and he was perfectly healthy. He just walked off the mailboat one day at St. Anthony, carrying all his belongings in a bag. When the doctor asked him why he had come, he said confidently, "To get learning."

Children like Percy, who lived too far from any school to "get learning" were the reason why the doctor had to start a boarding school in St. Anthony and another later much farther north in Cartwright.

In the logbook of the steamer, *Strathcona*, were to be found frequent notes like these:

"Hauled Gloucester schooner off rocks near Spotted Islands."

"Found *Mary G.* becalmed in Hare Bay and towed her out."

"Carried home crew of *Sally G.* wrecked off Cape Bauld. Salvaged cargo."

Going to the rescue of shipwrecked boats of every sort and size was all in the doctor's day's work. Skippers hailed him in fogs and in storms and among icebergs. They called upon him for a tow when he was hurrying on important business. Boats that were much heavier than the *Strathcona* asked the doctor to throw them a towline. Yet he never could bring himself to refuse "a brother in need, a brother who had done his best." So, to give still more help to the shipwrecked, Grenfell became an agent of Lloyd's of London, the company that handled all the marine insurance in Labrador.

Now and then a grimmer task than salvaging ships awaited him—the bringing to justice of men who had deliberately wrecked their boats in order to collect insurance for boat and cargo.

The perilous coast of Labrador had never been charted when Doctor Grenfell first came over. The waters were strewn with the bones of ships, and it was no wonder at all. Men sailed by guesses and by rhymes, such as,

> "When Joe Bett's pint you is abreast,
> Dane's Rock bears due west.
> West-Nor-west you must steer,
> Til' Brimstone Head do appear."

Sailing by guess and by rhyme along a shore that truly looked as if the Lord had "spent the sixth day throwing rocks at it!"

Almost as soon as he arrived down North, the doctor began charting the coast after his own fashion, taking soundings, drawing sketches to show the location of a particularly nasty reef or a jagged point of rock that he had discovered perhaps at the cost of a hole in his own boat, and making notes in his log.

Year after year he reminded the governor of the Colony that a survey of this coast was desperately needed. Nothing happened. Then came the great hurricane of 1908 that hurled ships upon the rocks literally by the hundreds and broke them into kindling wood. Governor Sir William MacGregor went into action. Together he and Dr. Grenfell worked by day and by night, turning the hospital of the *Strathcona* into an instrument room, traveling even as far north as Cape Chidley. The finished charts were accepted by the Royal Geographical Society and Doctor Grenfell received a prize from the society for his achievement.

Even harder did the doctor work to bring lights to the coast. The letters he sent to the Government at St. John's moved Parliament not at all. What did that doctor want now? He was always asking somebody to spend more money for Labrador. People down there had managed all right without lighthouses for years; they could get along a while longer.

Presently Grenfell stopped writing letters to the Government and began writing and talking to his friends. He described that dark coast, where no friendly lights flashed warnings to men in peril. He pictured a hundred boats waiting, waiting all night long outside Battle Harbor because they dared not come in after dark. He told of other boats more venturesome that had never sailed the seas again. He got the money for a lighthouse at Battle Harbor, and even an endowment sufficient to pay a lighthouse-keeper's salary. When the building materials had been all cut and sent north, the Government stepped in and said, "You can't build a lighthouse. No private individual can do that."

"All right. Here it is; you can put it up," was the answer.

That is how the Government of Newfoundland came to build its first lighthouse on the coast of Labrador.

"I can't get up; I ain't got no clothes."

"But where are the clothes you wore when you came to the hospital?"

"I borrowed them from a neighbor and my man took them back when he went home."

For women like this one, for babies dressed in trouser legs and flour sacks, for little girls like the one who walked to St. Anthony barefoot and with no coat over her cotton dress when the mercury stood at twenty below zero—for these and many others, Dr. Grenfell launched his secondhand clothing business. Collecting discarded clothes from friends, he sold them to men and women in exchange for work. A man, who found at a clothing

"Look at those blue-jerseyed Vikings"

center the warm sweater he needed, sawed wood for the *Strathcona's* engine, mended a komatik, or painted a boat in payment. A woman might buy a dress or a pair of shoes by doing some cleaning at the hospital.

Probably the happiest of all those who came to the clothing stations was the Indian who went home wearing a fox-huntsman's red broadcloth coat trimmed with gilt buttons.

Work that women could do at home, work for the old, the crippled, and the convalescent in a land where there was labor only for the hardy and vigorous—that was one of the great needs Doctor Grenfell had to fill. First, he set the women to hooking rugs, such as they made for their own homes only with more artistic patterns. Gradually, the Labrador hand industries developed. The people learned to do weaving, to make toys, to carve wood and ivory, and the things of beauty they turned out were sold in New York and other large cities.

Many a home was kept together through a bad fishing season by "mat money," as the doctor called it. And many a person who felt like a useless burden on others became a financial asset to his family. Old Uncle Ben, for example, with his hands crippled from arthritis, thought that all he could do was to sit around and wait for his time to be "runned up." Supplied with a foot treadle jigsaw, he began to turn out children's toys and to earn a tidy bit of money. One heard no more doleful talk about his being a "useless old man."

Sir Wilfred Grenfell

When Dr. Grenfell first came down North, he certainly never expected to be a farmer. Yet, if in his later years, someone had asked him "Of what piece of work are you especially proud?" he might well have replied, "Of raising eighteen-pound cabbages in Labrador." Why wouldn't anyone be elated over coaxing cabbages and turnips and potatoes into growing on that coast? Yes, he was proud of his demonstration farm in St. Anthony and of the fishermen who went and did likewise with seeds and plants from that farm. It's fun to do something that everyone says is impossible.

"There's no use wasting time trying to grow anything on rocks."

"There's earth enough for gardening even in Labrador if it is cleared and fertilized."

"The season's too short."

"I'll lengthen it with a greenhouse."

Thus he argued with doubters. Someone was always telling the doctor that his schemes were impractical.

Friends in the States sent the greenhouse down to him and he set to work, watering, weeding, and fighting white lice, potato bugs, and all the other insects that suddenly appeared when he planted their favorite edibles. A professor from Massachusetts Agricultural College came to the rescue, traveling north at his own expense to defend the doctor's farm against bugs and worms and lice.

Thoroughbred cows and pigs and sheep were raised on this farm. So were goats and rabbits. One thing led to

166

another. Before St. Anthony could raise domestic animals, the dog problem had to be dealt with. This time a man from the Animal Rescue League knew what to do. He provided the model kennels where St. Anthony huskies had such a home as no Labrador dog had ever known before. After the fame of these kennels had spread, the doctor offered to furnish wire fencing to those who would build roomy, comfortable quarters for their dogs.

Finally, after striving for years to bring it about, he succeeded in having a law passed that the huskies could not roam at will devouring what they pleased in the summertime. Their owners had to keep them shut up.

It is too long a tale to tell within book covers—the amazing story of how this doctor could turn his hand to one undertaking after another. Was there ever another man who could do quite so many different things? But *how* did he ever have the courage to tackle some of these ventures? How did he dare send for a sawmill and launch his cooperative mill, when he didn't even know what it looked like or how to set it up? Those pieces of metal were, he confessed, a Chinese puzzle to him. To be sure he set the log-hauling apparatus upside down. Yet somehow in time the thing was topside up, and giving work to sixty families. How did he dare start a fox farm or send for a herd of reindeer? Again, as in his earlier years, he looked at difficulties through the small end of the spyglass.

Another "Grenfell folly," said critics and enemies again and again of new ventures, and you may be sure there was plenty of criticism of a man who tried to bring about such drastic changes. Sometimes they were right, these critics. With so many different undertakings on foot, some were bound to be "follies." His attempt to introduce reindeer to Labrador and Newfoundland was a flat failure—and such a lot of trouble! The fishermen hunted them like ordinary game. The Government would not protect the herd. Then, in the midst of the experiment, Grenfell joined the Medical Corps and went to France to do what he could for the men in the trenches during the World War. The fox farm, too, was abandoned. Some of those cooperative stores were, as we have seen, costly experiments.

In a letter to his old friend, Captain Will Bartlett, written in Grenfell's later years, he looks back on himself as the "struggling young doctor, who had so many critics and who was never possessed of absolute wisdom." Today, probably his bitterest enemies would admit that the follies seem trifling when placed alongside all that has endured.

Of course, this work, as it grew and added one job after another, presently was too big for its parent, The Royal Mission. So there came into existence an International Grenfell Association, with branches in Great Britain, Ireland, Canada, and the United States.

Those who worked with Wilfred Grenfell were quite

out of breath at times. "Didn't he ever rest?" they asked. "Didn't he ever get tired?" A young man who sailed on his hospital boat, rising from sleep one morning just in time for eight-o'clock breakfast, discovered that Skipper Grenfell had not only stood early watch but, between turns at the wheel, had written a sixteen-page article. This was no unusual day either. He was up with the fishermen. Yet he was always ready to stand a night watch on shipboard or beside a sick bed. In early morning hours, late at night, between visits to cottages, between operations, he would work on a book, or an article he had promised to write for some magazine.

Did he have strength beyond that of most men? By no means. He was a man "very much in love with life." Enthusiasm for living carried him from one task to another. And he was spurred on by a never-failing conviction that in the eternal plan he had been assigned to a certain job. That job was Labrador.

CHAPTER EIGHTEEN

The Part That Was Drudgery

Down North work was play. The drudgery, the part Dr. Grenfell hated, was traveling about from city to city lecturing and asking people for contributions. Yet it had to be done. Every new plan meant just so much more time spent in raising money to carry it out.

When, in the fall of 1893, the twenty-eight-year-old doctor set out on his first real lecture trip, he felt as if high seas, ninety-mile gales, and the thirty-below-zero temperature of a Labrador winter were trifles beside what he was facing. Compared to such work, performing an operation by lamp light on a kitchen table was easy.

"How does a chap go about this sort of thing, anyway?" he asked the young Australian doctor who had come along with him. They were eating breakfast in a strange hotel in a strange city in Canada, a country neither of them knew except from maps. Nothing Wilfred Grenfell had learned at Marlborough, at the University, at the London Hospital seemed of any possible use to him now.

"Well, the first thing to do is to make an appointment with the Prime Minister."

Grenfell choked over a swallow of tea. "The *Prime Minister?* You certainly aren't serious."

"Never more serious in my life. Then we'll see the President of the Board of Trade, the General at the Garrison, and—"

"Oh, I say! That's just consecrated cheek."

"It *takes* cheek to raise money. You've got to begin with the people at the top."

Whew! This was going to be even worse than he had expected.

At the entrance to the office of the Prime Minister, Wilfred Grenfell felt much as he had that day when the *Albert* seemed to be crashing head-on into a towering iceberg. Only he was more scared today. What business had he barging in here—an unknown doctor working for a small northern mission? Then he thought of those two bare little hospitals perched on the rocks down there and all that he might do next year if he could get more equipment for them. He thought of that resolve made on the first voyage home—that the world should hear about Labrador.

"Up sails, Wilfred," he told himself, and strode in.

The young doctor must have made an extremely good impression on the high officials of the city. To his amazement, the Prime Minister, the President of the Board of Trade, and other prominent citizens were at once interested in the things he had to tell them. They organized a committee of friends of the Mission and agreed forthwith to support two Labrador hospital cots. What a wonderful start!

In the next city, Montreal, he had more nerve and was less worried about "consecrated cheek." Straight to Lord Strathcona, President of the Hudson's Bay Company, he went and there and then made for himself a friend who stood by him and Labrador as long as he lived. You see, Lord Strathcona had once been the boy Donald Smith, who had clambered over Labrador rocks and sailed in and out of Northern bays, and "jigged" for codfish, and he knew exactly what it was like to be poor. As chairman of a local committee he was a drawing card for the first meeting held in Montreal by Dr. Grenfell.

Ah, there was a man! He sent these two young men on a pleasure trip at his own expense clear across Canada to British Columbia, arranging to have them ride on the engine through the Rockies (how well he knew Grenfell already!) and entertaining them in his Winnipeg home. His first gift to the Mission was a fine steamboat, which the doctor promptly named *Sir Donald*. That hospital ship, the *Strathcona*, which became famous and in which Dr. Grenfell did so much traveling for years, was largely paid for by this generous friend.

The Labrador doctor was a success on lecture tours.

The Strathcona *went as far north as Cape Chidley*

Gatti-Casazza waits for Dr. Grenfell
to finish his speech

He had no impressive platform appearance. He spoke quietly, without any fireworks. Yet college boys would come to hear him in numbers that amazed the college authorities. Again and again people had to be turned away from a Grenfell meeting because all the standees the fire laws allowed had been admitted. Though he was no orator, how much he did have to say and with what enthusiasm he said it! In two minutes from the time he rose to speak, he could have a whole hallful of people down on the coast with him sailing on the *Strathcona*, dodging icebergs, skirting reefs, talking with Uncle Joe and Aunt Sally and little Pete.

"He has a genius for generating sympathy," Sir Frederick Treves said of him, "and he can simply wring tears from people's pocketbooks." This gift explains how he was able to get people to buy boats and sawmills, lighthouses and drydocks and almost anything under heaven that was badly needed down North.

What was he like on the platform? A plain man, plainly dressed, with no air of having explored far places or braved dangers. Only a coat of deep tan told of the battles he waged with gales and storms. Yet, when he began to speak you had to listen to him. And when he smiled, you would do anything for him that lay in your power.

Once when he was visiting a friend in New York, he had appointments with people "East side, West side, all around the town." "Did you have any trouble finding your way?" asked his host when finally he arrived back at his starting point after dark.

"Oh no!" was the cheerful reply. "I looked overhead and there was the North Star, and I steered by that."

He was all right as long as he could steer by a star. The great trouble with lecture tours was that he so seldom could get his bearings from the skies. There were railroad timetables to cope with and subways to endure and fixed—relentlessly fixed—appointments to be kept.

Trains played tricks on him, leaving before he was ready to go. "If Dr. Grenfell could miss a train or take the wrong one, he always did," said one who had had experience in managing his schedules.

"Are we going to Detroit or coming away from there?" he asked his wife one day in a state of complete confusion.

Again he absent-mindedly shook hands with an irate ticket taker at the gateway of a train instead of handing over his ticket.

Names played tricks on him, and he was supposed to remember hundreds of people's names. He could often recall almost everything else about a person but his name or where he lived. "I know just the man to be your new rector," he told a church warden. "What's his name?" asked the warden. "I don't remember." "Well, where does he come from?" "By jove! I've forgotten that, too, but he plays a bully game of squash."

He would forget the name of his host. A few minutes

after being introduced to a man and his wife, he would introduce them to each other.

Clothes played tricks on him. In Labrador he could live in an old sweater and baggy-kneed trousers or wear that faded football suit treasured ever since Oxford days, with an easy pair of moccasins on his feet. With all the other things on his mind, it was hard to remember about clothes. Just before one lecture, he complained to his wife that his feet hurt. She looked down at his shoes and burst out laughing. One foot sported a rubber-soled tennis shoe while the other was resplendent in patent leather.

How could a man who was used to steering by the North Star be expected to know that railroad station checkrooms were sometimes closed? That was how he happened to step off the train in a strange city one bright morning wearing white tie and tails. That was why he had to drape himself and pin himself with safety pins into a borrowed suit before he could give his lecture.

Time played tricks on him. Once he had taken an audience in imagination down on the coast and begun showing them his boats and his hospitals and his patients, time did not exist for him. A mere matter of making an eleven-twenty train on the opposite side of—say, New York or Chicago—was quickly and thoroughly forgotten.

Mrs. Grenfell would begin to fidget. Then she would write a little note, often in humorous tone, reminding him that the hands of the clock were still moving. If this failed, she might have to resort to removing stealthily some of the lantern slides from the box. This high-handed method of shortening a lecture he always discovered. *"Someone* seems to have taken out a number of my slides," he would remark blandly, as if he had no idea who could have done such a thing.

He hated to shorten a lecture, when he had much more to say. Yet no one realized better than he what difficulties and annoyances, what weariness of the flesh his wife's sense of time and her mindfulness of practical matters saved him.

Once at the Metropolitan Opera House in New York City he caused a behind-the-scenes explosion. The occasion was a benefit performance for the Grenfell Association, and Dr. Grenfell was called upon for a between-the-acts speech. The great audience in the many-tiered opera house listened to him as eagerly as they had to the glorious singing voices. In a few moments, they forgot that they were at the opera at all or even in New York City. The man on the stage was in Labrador, and so were they.

The signal bell sounded for the curtain to rise on the next act. The doctor went on talking. Frantic signaling began in the wings. The doctor went on talking. Now he was taking an imaginary dogsled ride to a patient. Behind the golden curtain Mr. Gatti-Casazza, the manager of the Opera Company, paced up and down "breathing out threatenings and slaughter." Lucretia Bori, who sang one of the leading roles, became hysterical. All unconscious of the crisis backstage, Grenfell steered the *Strathcona* into Battle Harbor with a head wind blowing.

The listeners were as unconscious of time as he was. It was the first time Wilfred Grenfell had ever competed with a prima donna or a golden-voiced tenor. Yet he certainly put up stiff competition.

Bores and inconsiderate people are the bane of every lecturer's life. As his fame grew, the askers of foolish questions, the long-winded after-lecture talkers, the autograph hunters increased. It was difficult for so kind and courteous a person to be rude to anyone. However, there were times when he could stand no more.

"Doctor, tell me what is your favorite hymn?" asked a lady.

He told her.

A little later the scatterbrained creature was back again putting exactly the same question.

This was too much. "Madam," was the reply this time, "my favorite hymn is 'Willie Had a Purple Monkey Climbing up a Tree.'"

One night he was so mobbed by questioners and autograph hunters that one of his staff had to come to his rescue. He emerged from the crush exclaiming indignantly, "At least in Labrador I'm the skipper of my own ship."

Formal occasions, such as big receptions and banquets, bored him. He confessed to having dozed off to sleep one time at a banquet and again in an opera box. Yet it was the wonder of a whole coast how he could travel all day to reach his patients and then stay up all night taking care of them. He could talk all night in Labrador, too, and he did once with two other doctors, while he laid plans for opening a boarding school at Cartwright.

To the men and women who entertained him in their homes, the Labrador doctor on lecture tour was a delight. He might be absent-minded. But what tales he could tell, and his own excitement over telling them was highly contagious. How he could play tennis! What a battle he fought out over the chess table! Not only did he talk with enthusiasm. He listened with equal enthusiasm. A rarity in human flesh is the person who does both of these things.

A man's work interested him. If this work were medicine or scientific research, then there were hours of talk. Yet he liked almost as much to hear people tell about jobs far different from his own. Their hobbies interested him. He would go into the darkroom with an amateur photographer and have a glorious time helping him develop pictures. A collection of almost any kind was the "beginning of a beautiful friendship." If the specialty proved to be birds or birds' eggs or moths or flowers, then was the collector a boon companion.

"Now where did you ever find this moth?"

"And this red burnet?"

"Ah! here's a flower that grows in only two or three places below the Arctic Circle. Did you know that?"

Thus he would talk.

What men believed about life interested him.

Only when the conversation turned to music or art did his attention wander a bit. Then he was out of his element. Grenfell's own family never let him forget a certain humiliating moment in his life. A well-known musician, who had come to St. Anthony, offered to give a piano recital at the Grenfell school. However, after trying out the piano, he changed his mind. "There's a note missing," he explained.

"Is it an important note?" asked the doctor.

Nor could he understand why everyone present except himself laughed.

Never did children enjoy a grown-up guest more than they did this man from Labrador. He could slip right into a child's world with no effort at all. You would find him down on the floor playing their own games with them, teaching them new games or acrobatic stunts.

"Which did you like better, the bishop or the doctor?" a man asked his children after a bishop and Dr. Grenfell had visited their home in quick succession.

"The doctor," was the prompt reply. "The bishop can't stand on his head."

Wilfred Grenfell might cordially dislike lecture tours, yet how much, how very much other people enjoyed his trips. Just as the hospital boat left a wake of smooth water in a ruffled Labrador sea, so this man left a wake of happiness behind him wherever he went.

CHAPTER NINETEEN

A "Big Toime" at St. Anthony

The *Strathcona II* rode at anchor in St. Anthony Harbor, bedecked from end to end with pennons like a pleasure boat. Alongside her lay H.M.S. *Wistaria*, come from St. John's with the Governor, Sir William Allardyce, and Lady Allardyce aboard. From every flagpole in the harbor there flew a British flag. Above the hospital, above Dr. Grenfell's house and the little teahouse fluttered two flags—Union Jack and Stars and Stripes. Back a way from the shore a reviewing stand, gay with bunting, waited for the guests of honor.

"'Twill be a big toime, the biggest toime there's ever been in St. Anthony," said the fishermen, as they ran up the flags on their schooners. Now and then one of them would glance proudly up beyond the bunting-draped stand to a new gray concrete building. It still didn't seem quite true—that their village had a hospital like that, fireproof, leakproof, galeproof, with up-to-date plumbing, electric lights, and all sorts of shining things

"The doctor's been knighted!"

that doctors love. How proud they were that it had all been done by their own boys. A local boy had supervised construction. Another had wired it for electricity, and still another had put in the plumbing. And today, July 25, 1927, the Governor was going to unveil the cornerstone. Ah, it was indeed a big time for the North coast!

Seen from an airplane, the village would have looked that morning like an ant hill that someone has just poked with a stick. The boys and girls at the Children's Home, smelling slightly of soap, were dressing up in best suits and gay dresses. *Left! Right! Left! Right!* That was the Girl Guides drilling. The Boy Scouts and the Church Lads Brigade were drilling too, in preparation for the landing of the Governor.

Within the new hospital, nurses were adjusting white headdresses and white veils and making sure that not a speck of dust marred the dazzling appearance of their uniforms. Dr. Curtis, the medical officer in charge of the hospital, went about seeing to it that everything in the place was in perfect working order. From the spotless new kitchen, delicious odors issued. The cook was baking for the supper party to be given that evening.

In the Industrial Building, the prettiest rugs and toys were exhibited, and men and women were sitting at looms and work benches ready to show off the skillfulness of their hands.

Dr. Grenfell was everywhere, wearing a flower in his

buttonhole and a smile on his face that eclipsed all the other smiles in town. Mrs. Grenfell, busy arranging for a luncheon party at her house in honor of the Governor and his Lady, looked as if her thoughts were extremely pleasant. If anyone had had time that morning to watch the Grenfells closely, he might have seen them exchanging glances as much as to say, "We know something that these people don't know yet." Sir William and Lady Allardyce were the only persons who shared the secret.

From one of the buildings, where the Community Club were rehearsing for their concert, floated the strains of the Newfoundland National Anthem. The doctor stood still for a moment and listened:

> "When sun rays crown thy pine-clad hills
> And summer spreads her hand
> When silvern voices tune thy rills
> We love thee, smiling land."

"We love thee, smiling land," he hummed to himself a little off key.

> "When blinding storm gusts fret thy shore
> And wild waves lash thy strand,
> Though spin drift swirl and tempest roar,
> We love thee, windswept land."

As for him, he loved it best when the winds blew and the "wild waves lashed the strand." Fierce struggles to bring his ship to port through storms, wild nights when the winds twisted the trees and made them cry out— those were the best times of all. Then Newfoundland was a man's land, an explorer's land.

A whistle blew from down the harbor. A chorus of whistles answered. "It's the *Silver City!*" "The *Silver City's* come," rang from one end of the village to the other, and men, women, and children began trooping to the dock. This boat was bringing from the nearest railroad station miles away a group of distinguished guests— Admiral Sir James Startin from England, representing the British branch of the Grenfell Association, Judge Morris, an official representative of the Newfoundland Government, and high dignitaries from the United States and Canada.

Dr. Grenfell was on the dock to welcome them. "This is a great day for you, Doctor." "You must be feeling mighty proud today," said the visitors as they went up the steps of that new eight-hundred-bed hospital. Of course the man who had dreamed about this building for years was proud. It seemed as if he must be still dreaming, as he showed off his new operating room. "If you had ever operated on a woman upon a kitchen table, while her husband held a kerosene lamp for you to see by, if you'd ever had to thaw out a frozen board before you could splint a boy's broken leg, then you would know how I feel today," he told them.

"We can imagine," they said. Yet not one of them,

not even the doctors, could quite appreciate how much this hospital meant to Wilfred Grenfell.

"And here's our almost-new Children's Home built three years ago." He was nearly as proud of this building as of the brand-new hospital. Didn't it have *four bathrooms*, a sun porch, a playroom that a child anywhere would think was a fine place to play in, and a library? Somehow this place always reminded him of Prince Pomiuk, the son of an Eskimo chief whom he had found twenty years ago lying on the rocks in a far-north village, forlorn, neglected, and dying. This dark-skinned little boy was the first child he had ever "adopted," and none had ever taken the place of "the happy prince," as everyone called him.

At one-thirty sharp, the band began to play and the Governor General, in his gold-braided dress uniform, and the Governor's Lady in a beautiful gown and a big hat, came ashore to take their places on the reviewing stand. The boys and girls marched for Their Excellencies. Then the speeches began. Now it was Dr. Grenfell's turn just to sit back and listen while *other* people talked about his work. Seldom did he have a chance to do this.

"During more than a third of a century Grenfell has worked with wholehearted devotion and self-effacement," said the Governor.

A third of a century! The time sounded long, when you put it that way. Yet how short it really seemed.

"More than thirty years since the *Albert* first sailed,"— that sounded shorter. Why, it was only yesterday that he had put in at Domino Run for the first time. "Devotion?" Yes. "Self-effacement?" Never. Thus ran the doctor's thoughts as he listened.

Now Sir William was telling the story of that first patient dying in a dark sod hut and of the man in the rowboat who asked, "Be you a real doctor?" That *did* seem a long time ago. One seldom saw a Labrador liveyere in rags today, and men as sick as that wretched man in the hut now found care in a hospital. Life was pleasant to look back upon, with all its difficulties and disappointments, when at the end of thirty years you could see that the people along a whole stretch of coast were better off and happier because you had not "passed by on the other side."

Presently the hospital cornerstone was unveiled, the words of dedication were spoken, and the new building was officially opened by the Governor. Grenfell sat and smiled at his own thoughts. How few people present half knew what a change this was from the old building. That old wooden hospital built of green lumber had been like a sieve in winter winds. And how it had shown its age of late! For the last few months, the nurses had had to put up umbrellas over the patients' beds when there was a heavy rain. He could smile about that leaky roof now.

His Excellency finished speaking and made an impressive pause. Then he unfolded a piece of paper and started to read. "His Majesty, the King, has been graciously pleased," rang out Sir William's voice, "to confer the honor of Knight Commander of St. Michael and St. George on Dr. Grenfell."

The great secret was out.

The Grenfells had been told the afternoon before, when they took tea with the Governor and his Lady on the *Wistaria,* and for nearly twenty-four hours had kept the news to themselves.

A great roar of applause went up. It echoed back from the farther side of St. Anthony harbor. Still only a few people knew exactly what the announcement meant, except that their doctor was being honored in some way by his king. Not till Admiral Startin called for "three long cheers for Sir Wilfred Thomason Grenfell, K.C.M.G." and then "three cheers for Lady Grenfell" did everybody realize what had happened. Then the whispers and the murmurs from the crowd were like the sound of a great sea. "The doctor's been knighted! The doctor's been knighted!"

The first thing Dr. Grenfell worried over was whether this honor would separate him from the people. "I only pray," he wrote to a friend, "that this tag to my name instead of 'the doctor' that I have loved so well may make no barrier between myself and any friends on this coast." Far better to have no title if it were to come between him and them.

He need not have been anxious. The "Sir" before his name made no difference to others because it made no difference to him. He was the same modest, friendly doctor they had known ever since the first day he landed on their coast. The people down North liked to call him Sir Wilfred, but he was still just their doctor.

The knighthood received on that summer day in 1927 came as a climax to honors that had been piling up for years. Already, had he chosen to do so, he could have placed a long row of letters after his name. Twenty years earlier, on May Day, he had stood up in a red robe before an almost overwhelming assemblage of notables and received an honorary degree in medicine from Oxford University, where he had studied for only one term. It was the first time in the hoary history of ancient Oxford that anyone had been given this degree. Sometimes he could still hear the opening words of the Latin speech delivered that day, "A citizen of Britain is before you, once a student in this University, now better known to the people of the New World than to our own."

Grenfell was proud of the honor, but it was like him to hate wearing the red academic robe. "It makes me feel like a sunset," he said. Yet he would put on an old gaily-striped Oxford football blazer whenever he had a chance.

One university and college after another bestowed honors upon the Labrador doctor—McGill, Harvard, Williams, Middlebury, Bowdoin, Berea in the Kentucky mountains, to which he had sent many Labrador boys and girls, and a number of others. The Royal College of Surgeons of England made him a Fellow. So did the American College of Surgeons. Then there were many medals. The one that probably gave him the greatest pleasure was the Livingstone Gold Medal, presented by the Royal Scottish Geographical Society. Hadn't Dr. Livingstone been one of his special heroes ever since he could remember?

Strange, wasn't it, how his life turned out? A young doctor in his twenties puts honor and fame behind him. At least he must have thought he was doing just that when in 1892 he set out to doctor unknown fishermen on an unknown coast. "Where was Labrador?" people asked him. "Oh yes, away north where the Eskimos lived." "Did he ever see a white man?" "Was the ground frozen all the year round?"

So, feeling somewhat shy and out of his element, he had set out to tell people what Labrador was really like and how they could help the coast to come into its own. To reach a still larger audience, he began to write about that coast—books, magazine articles and stories. And lo! the Labrador doctor became famous. What a good joke on Wilfred Grenfell!

Now he was Sir Wilfred Grenfell and could place after his name the title, Knight Commander of Saint Michael and Saint George. To receive a "birthday honor" from his king moved him deeply, as it would any Englishman. Yet, beyond personal pride, was another reason why his face was alight with happiness on July 25, 1927. This title would clear away as if by magic, many obstacles that had been placed in his path. Had he been a Knight years ago, instead of "that queer English doctor who hobnobbed with fishermen as if he were one himself," how much more quickly the Newfoundland Government would have built the lighthouses he asked for and granted other urgent requests he made. His many critics, who had shrugged their shoulders and labeled this plan and that plan as "another Grenfell folly" would be in much less of a hurry now to dismiss a pet scheme as a "Sir Wilfred Grenfell folly." Of course it's silly for people to be like that. Yet 'tis the way of the world.

Once satisfied that a handle to his name would change his relationship with old Labrador friends not a bit, the newly-knighted doctor was well content. How delighted he was when someone, probably a Wop, first shortened the "Sir Wilfred" to a flip and affectionate "Sir Wilf!"

There was one person who was disappointed by the simplicity of this modern knight. Tearfully a little boy confided to Lady Grenfell one day, "I have just shaken hands with a real knight, but he left his armor at home."

That was a great day in the summer of 1928 when Sir Wilfred went to London to Buckingham Palace and received from the hands of King George V the jeweled insignia of the Order of St. Michael and St. George. This was not the first time the King had received the

Labrador doctor. For years he had been interested in the great work of healing and helping others that this one of his subjects was building in a small corner of the Empire. As for Queen Mary, she had heard about Dr. Grenfell and Labrador thirty-five years ago when as a young lady she cabled to St. John's, Newfoundland, that she would be pleased to have a certain small steam launch bear her name—*Princess May*.

CHAPTER TWENTY

"Tied Up to a Wharf"

"It seems to me now as if she must be just fretting cruelly at being tied up to a wharf while the season of open water is passing away," Grenfell wrote in his logbook when once the *Strathcona* lay idle and useless for months waiting for new boilers. "She seems to be calling me to come and let her away to her work once more."

These imaginings about a disabled boat were a perfect description of how he felt years later. At sixty-nine he was forced to retire from active duty on the coast, and nothing that had ever happened to him was quite so hard to accept. Why, every wind that blew down from the North called, "Come back." Each return of spring reminded him that the ice had gone out of Labrador harbors and it was time to set out in his floating hospital. The cool breath of September told him that the "season of open water is passing away." As for the sight of a winter snowstorm, it made him ache to hop onto a

191

komatik, crack his whip, and call "Haul up!" to a team of dogs.

These doctors that told him he must be careful—how miserable they made life for him! He too made life difficult for the doctors. As for Lady Grenfell, who tried so hard to look after him, he kept her in a state of almost constant anxiety.

The trouble was that Sir Wilfred's heart had finally rebelled and was insisting on being given an easier life. It had certainly earned a rest. That heart had pounded steadily on through morning dips in ice water, long night watches on the *Strathcona*, breathless races on snowshoes to patients, strenuous games of tennis and squash, and all through one long, bitter cold night on an icepan, when many another heart would have given up the struggle in a few hours.

Yet who can blame a Labrador doctor and a master mariner for fretting at being "tied up to wharf"? "Rest," said the doctors. Rest! He scarcely knew what the word meant. To live—so far as he was concerned—was to be active. His idea of hell was a place where there was nothing to do, and his heaven was an unexplored region of wide plains, lofty mountains, and restless seas, where "we shall run and not be weary."

No wonder he broke away from his moorings again and again. Ordered to Battle Creek Sanatorium for a rest, he turned the trip out to Michigan into a lecture tour. Once when a stay in a hospital had been forced upon him, he actually climbed out of a window and came home.

"You'll have to give up the trip, Sir Wilfred," said the doctor firmly one winter after a strenuous season of lecturing had been planned. "You aren't fit to travel."

His secretary proceeded to cancel all lecture engagements. She only made for herself a lot of extra work.

"Why, I've never broken a lecture engagement in my life," declared Grenfell indignantly. This was true. He never had, and he didn't this time. The lectures were all given, even though the speaker had to make some of them sitting down instead of on his feet.

Sometimes his heart protested so emphatically that it could not be ignored. There was a period when the Labrador doctor had not only to rest but to refuse himself to guests, even to close friends. Still he made a joke of that. "I've retired to my palace," said he. "The Palace" was a small wooden cottage built a little away from Kinloch House, the unpretentious white house that was now the Grenfell summer home.

A newspaper man, taking the remark literally, reported that "Sir Wilfred Grenfell was spending the summer in his palace on Lake Champlain." The truth would have made better copy, with some such heading as, "A Knight in a Cottage."

It was a beautiful spot, that farm on the shores of the lake, with a view of the Adirondack Mountains on one side and the Green Mountains on the other. Yet a land-locked lake is not the sea. How quickly and how gladly he would have exchanged its green, flower-strewn shores for the barest, grayest rocks of Labrador.

When he was able to deafen his ears to the call of the North, life could be fun on a lake. There was Kimmie, the black cocker spaniel his wife gave him, so like Jack that it seemed sometimes as if this little fellow had been his foot warmer that night out in the middle of Hare Bay on an icepan. The motorboat, sent all the way from St. Anthony, made him feel more at home in Vermont. A friend of his who spent her vacations on Lake Champlain tells of sighting him put-putting across the lake. He waved gaily, patted the side of the little boat, as one might pat a favorite horse, and called out, "It's my old boat from down North."

It looked for a while as if the *Petrel* would arrive before a dock could be built to receive her. "I'll build one myself," threatened Sir Wilfred, knowing all too well that he could lift rocks and timbers no more. The delay was maddening. Then a seeming miracle took place.

Two boys off on a summer vacation trip came speeding along Route 7 in Vermont.

"Sir Wilfred Grenfell, that Labrador doctor, has a place around here somewhere. Why don't we look him up?" suggested College Boy Number One.

"Do you know the guy?" asked Number Two.

"No, but we can just drop around and introduce ourselves. He likes college boys."

So, with "consecrated cheek," the two young men walked up the steps of Kinloch House, rang the bell, and asked to see Sir Wilfred.

Lady Grenfell wanted to tell these cheeky strangers that her husband could not be disturbed. He thought differently. In fact that was a matter about which they seldom agreed. He did not want to shut himself away from people. To love his neighbor was as natural to him as breathing. Some "neighbors" might take advantage of his friendliness. They might outstay their welcome. Yet he never wanted to turn them away without a greeting, and sometimes one "entertained angels unawares."

This proved to be one of those times. "You two chaps are like an answer to prayer," said "Tom Sawyer" Grenfell, smiling one of his memorable smiles and shaking their hands. "I've been itching to build a dock for the boat they're sending down from Newfoundland, but the doctor says, 'NO.'"

Before they quite knew what was happening, the young men felt irresistibly impelled to put on their shorts, wade into the lake, and start on a back-breaking job.

"What fun!" said College Boy Number One, quite unconscious of the blisters he was raising on his hands.

"Absolutely," agreed Number Two. "I'm mighty glad we stopped."

"They're as good Wops as any I ever had," reported Grenfell triumphantly.

He still worked hard summer and winter, except when literally forced to rest. There remained so much to do, and the time grew short. Always his plans for the North coast ran ahead of what any collection of human beings could accomplish. He wanted to see more farms down there, more greenhouses, more schools, more hospitals as complete and modern as the St. Anthony hospital. There should be airplane service to carry supplies quickly and easily even to the northernmost villages.

Tourists were beginning to discover the joys of a cruise along that coast. Yet only a beginning had been made in advertising its beauties. So he kept on adding to his lantern slides and traveling about telling of this land that was so especially his own. He went to teas and opened bazaars and sales at summer hotels, whether he felt like it or not, to help the sale of the beautiful things Labrador people had learned to make.

There was one more voyage to St. Anthony for Sir Wilfred—in 1939. The errand was a sad one. He was carrying out Lady Grenfell's last wish, that her ashes be buried on Fox Farm Hill near the home she had come to as a bride. So he went back home once more.

The people of St. Anthony put up a welcome arch decked with green boughs of spruce and balsam. The little boats came winging and chugging and put-putting into the harbor. The news was carried from boat to boat and from cottage to cottage—"The doctor's 'ere. 'E's come back." The smiles on their faces were a joy to see,

The doctor's last visit to Labrador

and their sympathy and affection were like a soothing balm poured upon a wound.

In spite of his sadness, this visit held for him moments that were "truly like old days." One old friend invited him to share the little cabin on his fishing schooner. What could possibly have suited him better? The "hot tea and good loaf and butter" eaten at a friend's cottage tasted as good as "any refreshment at Delmonico's or at Buckingham Palace, especially when fortified by some fresh fried fat codfish and kindly greetings."

At Conche, a near-by village, the men took down their old muzzle-loading, barreled guns and fired a salute to the man who was still "their doctor."

It was pleasant to set out on the Mission boat *Northern Messenger*. Yet how "resentfully he accepted a pilot." 'Twas hard not to steer his own boat, after all the sporting chances he had taken afloat. Pushing along through the fog was like the old days, and how natural it was to be hailed by a man in a fishing boat and summoned to see a boy who had been unconscious for two days. "He's fifteen and our only hope," said the worried father.

A talk with an old friend who had been Chief Justice of the Supreme Court brought back memories of his days as a magistrate. To see the men who had saved his life on Hare Bay thirty-one years before was to shiver in recollection of an icy wind blowing across that bay. "We ne'er thought that night we'd be seeing you in this world again," they told him as they had so many times before.

It was pleasant to go back to Red Bay where that small band of desperate fishermen had started the first cooperative.

"The lovely colored cliffs," a "very remarkable long iceberg," the herring "splashing their tails out of the sea"—all these things he noticed with fresh enjoyment and, getting out sketchbook and water colors, he put them down on paper.

How good to see the work going busily on as it used to! The sick were being healed. He could still glow with pride at the sight of the St. Anthony hospital and at the thought that it had been given an A-1 rating by the American College of Surgeons. The farms were flourishing and spreading all the time. It seemed as if the cabbages were bigger than ever. The Industrial Building resounded with the clatter of looms and the sound of jigsaws as when last he was here. The children at the home and in the Grenfell School were happy and healthy. At seventy-four, the Labrador doctor was as keenly interested in every detail as he had ever been.

Yet this home-coming made him realize with painful vividness one great change. He was not the pilot of the ship now. He had turned over the wheel to others.

CHAPTER TWENTY-ONE

Last Voyage

The days seemed longer after Lady Grenfell was gone. The man whose work and play she had shared so completely never doubted that he and Anne would be together again. Yet he missed her so now. It would have been easier, far easier, to go on by himself, if only he could have spent those last years at home among his fishermen. Even that cheerfulness that seemed an inseparable part of him gave way at times. To be active and to be helping other people—these two things were as necessary to his happiness as breathing is to life.

"I'd like," he told a friend, "to go down to New York City to the Lower East Side and start a social settlement or health center there." If he couldn't stand work in a northern climate any longer, he wanted to do something just as much of a service to others, just as active, somewhere else. Yet he knew that at seventy such a plan was out of the question.

Well, there was still much to do for his fishermen

199

right where he was. As in the past, work and more work was his cure for the doldrums. So he went on lecturing and "wringing tears from people's pocketbooks." He enjoyed dropping in and helping sales along at the Dog Team Tavern, near his Vermont home. This summer inn had been started by his wife as an outlet for Labrador hand-work. The small unused chapel next door to it he turned into a Labrador museum. That was good fun —to bring together his Labrador trophies in one place. Here were pictures, an old komatik, the harness that his dogs had worn on that memorable Sunday in 1908, snowshoes, a costume showing "what the well-dressed man" will wear on a dog-sledge, specimens of Northern birds and Northern minerals. Here he gave lantern lectures to summer tourists. Thus he kept busy. And none but members of his family and his closest friends suspected that Sir Wilfred of the Radiant Smile was often lonely and always a little homesick.

A schoolgirl, who visited him the summer before he died, describes him thus: * "He was tall and tanned, with a slim, straight figure that belied his seventy-five years. His smile was the sweetest I had ever seen, and his friendly blue eyes shone and crinkled at the edges. As Mother and he discussed old times in Labrador I was completely won over by his hearty laugh and boyish grin."

* "Glimpses of a Great Man," by Patricia Knapp, from *The Triangle,* published by the Emma Willard School.

Last Voyage

She understood why people said there never was another man who had so many friends.

On the first evening of her visit, he played Chinese checkers with her and "complicated the game till it was too hard for her." Next morning she was "awakened by an eerie howling. Terrified at first, I was much relieved to hear Sir Wilfred saying, 'Sing, Kimmie boy, sing!' Kim was Sir Wilfred's cocker spaniel. The night before I had watched him beg, roll over, play dead, take a handkerchief from Sir Wilfred's pocket, and do any number of tricks, but when I heard him sing, I, like Sir Wilfred, was sure of his super-animal qualities.

"Before we started breakfast, Sir Wilfred read, as always, out of a book which his wife had compiled just before she died. It contained inspirational verses and bits of philosophy. He said it not only started him out right for the day, but that it made him seem nearer to his wife. Then we knelt before our chairs while Sir Wilfred said a prayer. After breakfast we all went to church. It was a small church in which every voice counted. Sir Wilfred's was loud, sincere, and a bit off key. . . .

"Sunday night was the part of my visit I enjoyed most. . . . He talked about his defeats and disappointments, his hopes and achievements. He said, as he later wrote me, that to follow Christ was an invitation never to get weary of being alive, and that Christ lived with those who worked. He told me how he read his Bible, marked it with his own observations, and then often gave it away to someone who begged for it. He even seemed to value my opinions on religion and philosophy. . . .

"He worked tirelessly all afternoon, but still had time to learn to play croquet, becoming so proficient that he nearly beat us all. Sir Wilfred, who had always excelled in sports, particularly football, often remarked how furious he was because he had recently had to give up tennis. He still wore his tennis shoes and an old blazer which he had won for athletic prowess when he was young. . . .

". . . I shall never forget him, nor will anyone who has ever shaken his hand."

That amazing zest for life he was born with stood him in good stead now. The world was still full of fascinating things. He could discover the first flowers of spring with all the delight a child feels. "I get excited when I win," he wrote to a friend about croquet. Chess, which he had played for years whenever he found a worthy opponent, was still a favorite indoor sport. There were birds in Vermont that were new to him. He gathered specimens of their eggs—as much of a collector as he had ever been. Sometimes he would make a sketch or a water-color painting of a bird or a bird's nest.

His children, now grown up, spent their vacations with him. In winter he took trips south, finding old friends and new friends wherever he went. Of course the best part of a stay in Florida was the fishing.

Last Voyage

When he was forced just to loaf, what memories were Sir Wilfred's to enjoy! A motion picture camera in his brain would unwind at his bidding reel after reel. Black shadows of dogs against moonlit snow. An ice palace, ghostly under the moon, dazzling-bright under the sun. Women pouring bright red wild cranberries into a white sheet in the wind, to winnow out stems and leaves. Fishing schooners in a fleet like a flock of giant sea birds. A long procession of men, women, and children trooping off the *Prospero* at St. Anthony and up the path to the hospital—some swathed in bandages, some limping, some groping in the darkness of the blind. The same procession going home again, so changed. Children playing in the schoolyard.

Those pictures had sound effects, too. There was the *Strathcona's* whistle! It sounded just the way a little boy once described it. "She can whistle two ways; the first time she squeals and the second time she bawls nearly like a cow." "Rur-rup! Rur-rup!" Now the *Strathcona* was in for it. She had landed on a reef. Dogs howled under the stars. Winds roared in the woods. A young man pulled out and pushed together the folds of an accordion as he sang:

"She tore her flannel petticoat
To make mittens for me hands
Saying, 'I can't see my true love freeze,
On the Banks of Newfoundland.' "

203

Best of all was the voice of a fisherman greeting him, "I give ye kindly welcome, doctor."

Above and beyond the voices, the winds and the howls of dogs was always another sound—the "swish-boom! swish-boom!" of waves breaking against unyielding rocks.

He must have thought often of England during the last years of his life, of England under fire. National selfishness, the barriers that nations erected between one another—these were things he had again and again cried out against. How long would it be before men learned that they must cooperate to survive? After a trip around the world in 1928, he had said, "No nation, or man, can live to themselves without injuring themselves as well as all the world." It was a prophecy of what came to pass.

The end came gently, on an afternoon in October, just when the Vermont woods blazed defiance of approaching winter. Wearing that favorite Oxford blazer, he played croquet with a friend and then went up to his room for a nap before dinner.

He was tired. Tired after two or three games of croquet! How humiliating! A little sleep would fix him up. As he drowsed off, the boom of surf on Labrador shores was in his ears.

Ah! How sweet, how heavenly sweet, the cool Northern air smelled! Here was the *Strathcona II* waiting for him. It was good to be on that "rolling ark of mercy" again. One of his favorite Wops had given her that name. "Up sails! Up sails! A fair wind's blowing."

That night the news was flashed around the world that Sir Wilfred Grenfell had embarked on his last voyage. It was carried to the North coast by the telegraph line and the wireless stations he had brought to those shores. Little boats went in and out of the faraway coves and runs with word that " 't doctor was dead." The fishermen wept without shame. Even the young children, who had never seen Sir Wilfred, were sad, for they had heard again and again about this great doctor. He must have been, they thought, the kindest man in the whole world.

Men mourned his passing in Eskimo villages just below the Arctic Sea and far beneath the equator in New Zealand. East and West, thousands of men and women who had been doctors, nurses, and teachers in Labrador or had helped the Labrador doctor in some way, and scores of others who had been close friends of his were saddened at the thought that they would never feel his handclasp or see that unforgettable smile again. Yet a deep gratitude filled them because they had known one such man in a lifetime. Thousands of others, who had admired him from the distance, perhaps from far back in a lecture hall or just as readers of his books, these, too, felt that they had lost someone the like of whom would never pass their way again.

On July 25, 1941, the flags of St. Anthony were

hauled down to half mast, while a long procession of men, women, and children climbed to the top of Fox Farm Hill. The procession was led by boys and girls from the Children's Home, headed by the oldest boy in the home who carried the ashes of Sir Wilfred Grenfell. In the rear an old lady of seventy hobbled along with the help of a crutch and a cane. Although she had broken her hip the winter before, she declared that nothing could keep her from paying her respects to this old friend.

Sky and sea were as blue and white, the cliffs as pink, and the woods as green as on that August day in 1892 when the young doctor first looked upon the northern coast with all the joy and wonder of a discoverer. Under the great boulder on the hilltop, in a grave lined with wild iris, beside the grave of Lady Grenfell, they placed his ashes. "For All the Saints Who from their Labors Rest," rang out the voices of old and young. "Rest?" whispered the spruces and pine trees. Would the man who had planted with his own hands this whole hilltop of trees ever consent just to rest?

The little company of friends were silent as they went back down the hill. Their thoughts had been perfectly expressed by another old friend of Sir Wilfred's—the customs officer at Port au Bras, Newfoundland, who said, "He did more for this coast than anybody ever did, even old John Cabot that discovered it, and more than anybody ever will again."

Last Voyage

Set into the boulder above Sir Wilfred's grave is a bronze tablet that bears this inscription—

> In loving memory of
> Wilfred Thomason Grenfell
> Born—February 28, 1865
> Died—October 9, 1940
> "Life is a field of honor"

Better than anyone else could possibly express it did Sir Wilfred sum up his own life when he said those words—

"Life is a field of honor, and what we give to it is the measure of what we get out of it."

CPSIA information can be obtained
at www.ICGtesting.com
Printed in the USA
LVOW13s0037300517

536192LV00034B/1785/P

9 781163 134337